THE BURGLAR CAUGHT BY A SKELETON AND OTHER SINGULAR TALES FROM THE VICTORIAN PRESS

JEREMY CLAY

ICON

This edition published in the UK in 2014 by
Icon Books Ltd, Omnibus Business Centre,
39–41 North Road, London N7 9DP
email: info@iconbooks.com
www.iconbooks.com

Originally published in the UK in 2013 by Icon Books Ltd

Sold in the UK, Europe and Asia
by Faber & Faber Ltd, Bloomsbury House,
74–77 Great Russell Street,
London WC1B 3DA or their agents

Distributed in the UK, Europe and Asia
by TBS Ltd, TBS Distribution Centre, Colchester Road,
Frating Green, Colchester CO7 7DW

Distributed in India by Penguin Books India,
7th Floor, Infinity Tower – C, DLF Cyber City,
Gurgaon 122002, Haryana

Distributed in South Africa by Jonathan Ball,
Office B4, The District, 41 Sir Lowry Road, Woodstock 7925

Distributed in Australia and New Zealand
by Allen & Unwin Pty Ltd, PO Box 8500,
83 Alexander Street, Crows Nest, NSW 2065

Distributed in Canada by Publishers Group Canada,
76 Stafford Street, Unit 300, Toronto, Ontario M6J 2S1

ISBN: 978-184831-737-6

Typeset in Adobe Caslon by Marie Doherty
Printed and bound in the UK by Clays Ltd, St Ives plc

CONTENTS

About the author

Jeremy Clay is a journalist who has worked in newspapers for twenty years. He lives in Leicester with his family, and a dog with a passing resemblance to Denis Healey.

*To Lilia Flynn, who loved history, and her daughter Liz,
who couldn't care less for it, but helped all the same.*

INTRODUCTION

On a summer's evening in 1837, in a room in one of the fanci-
est addresses in all of London, a teenage girl called Alexandrina
sat down with her diary.

'Up at 6am', she wrote. 'Uncle William the Fourth died
in the night. That makes me the Queen. Huh! Spent the
afternoon with a load of lords talking about royal stuff. Tea.
Crown-fitting. Bed. PS Think I'll call myself Victoria. It'll look
better on pub signs.'

I paraphrase, but you get the picture: June 20, 1837 was
quite a to-do for the eighteen-year-old. And what with one
thing and another, it's likely the new Queen of the United
Kingdom of Great Britain and Ireland never found a spare
moment to flick through the papers.

What did she miss that day? Oh, you know. The usual. A
pub landlord who drowned himself in 500 gallons of beer. A
punch-up between rival teetotallers at a temperance meeting.
A parcel of £400 sent between two Cumbrian towns, delivered
35 years late. A chap who, for no readily discernible reason, had
embarked on a mission to walk 1,250 miles in 1,000 hours, all
along the same small stretch of road. The usual unusual.

Fast-forward 63 years to January 22, 1901, and Queen
Victoria found herself otherwise engaged once more, this time
with the even more pressing business of dying. Let's assume she
skipped the papers again and never read that a gaggle of girls
had been openly sold by auction on the streets of San Francisco
or that … well, actually that was pretty much it for striking

stories that day. The press, understandably, was rather preoccupied with the fading health of the monarch, which due to the journalistic quirks of the era unfolded in a series of updates in the same editions, popping up again and again from page to page just when you thought it was all done, like a breakfast-time flare-up of last night's lovers' tiff.

So: June 20, 1837 and January 22, 1901. Remember those dates, they're important. Actually, scrub that. They're not. Forget them. Like a spray of urine from a territorial tom cat, they merely mark the boundaries of our interest.

The Victorian age, as any dog-eared school history textbook will confirm, was a time of tumultuous change, and that was as true for journalism as it was for society as a whole.

From rude beginnings in the days of mud-slinging pamphlets and thunderous broadsides, newspapers had worked themselves into the foundations of British society. Gone was the buccaneering spirit of the freewheeling early days, when the *Leicester Journal*, for instance, for want of anything else to print, serialised the Book of Genesis. In its place came an increasing professionalism; a little less thrillingly unpredictable maybe, but far more reliable.

In the meantime, newspapers were gorging themselves on the fruits of the age of innovation. Railways sped up delivery of papers. Telegraph wires meant news travelled ever faster. The spread of steam presses accelerated the printing process. Gas and eventually electric lighting meant people could read long into the evening rather than just trudging off to bed in the gathering gloom. All this, and the stamp duty that was designed to shackle the press was finally abolished too, alongside taxes on paper and advertising. Cover prices tumbled and readership swelled, as an increasingly literate and politicised nation with a voracious appetite for shock, scandal and sport – plus a mystifyingly high tolerance for dreary reports of ceremonial dinners – provided a ready, hungry market for news.

In these sunny conditions, journalism flourished. In 1837, according to a tally in the bracingly titled *Pigot and Co.'s National Commercial Directory of the Whole of Scotland, and of the Isle of Man with a General Alphabetical List of the Nobility, Gentry and Clergy of Scotland* – breathe here, please – there were 346 titles publishing in Britain and 68 more in Ireland. Names like the *Hue and Cry* and the *Sheffield Iris* may not have stayed the course, but by 1901 the snappier-sounding *Mitchell's Newspaper Press Directory* listed 2,488 papers in production.

They're curious things, Victorian newspapers, and not simply because a queen could be gravely ill on page two of your *Evening Telegraph* and gravely dead by page three.

At first glance, they seem as glum and forbidding as the stereotype of the thin-lipped, hidebound, naked-table-leg-abhorring people they served.

Barring a few honourable exceptions – most notably the skittish, yahooing *Illustrated Police News* – the front page is surrendered to the classifieds. From a hat for your head to shoes for your feet, with elixirs for the taming of fierce flatulence for the regrettable bit between, they advertise everything and anything, including the cold, commercial instincts of the publisher.

Turn over, and things improve, but only marginally. Here, at last, is some news, but it's the devil's own job picking it out. There are few illustrations, by and large. Paragraphs run on and on, and then on some more. Columns can be thin or wide, so long as they're fit to burst. Pages are busier than a grave-digger in a flu pandemic. From the *John O'Groat Journal* to the *Royal Cornwall Gazette*, newspapers look as if they were produced by a man who found the design for the average book of logarithms unduly frivolous. It's a wonder Reader's Migraine didn't join Cobbler's Femur and Chimney Sweep's Scrotum in the roll-call of Victorian ailments.

The remedy, you'd think, would be found in headlines; something to break up the page and offer a little breathing room amid the crush. All too often, though, they simply squeeze up on the same line as the intros, like travelling salesmen forced to share the last bed at a B&B. Starved of space to shine, headline-writing is prosaic and functional. There's no hint of the giddy wordplay that's the calling card of the modern-day British press. Victorian sub-editors, it seems, could spend the working week blithely adding headings like 'A Strange Story' or 'A Remarkable Tale' to near enough every article they encountered (although a tip of the hat to whoever came up with the splendidly dismissive 'More French Insolence' for a piece in the *Morning Post* in 1839).

If the headlines lack a little zip, some of the journalism they introduce is positively deathly. I have before me an 1890 article from the influential weekly *The Graphic*, on the already pulse-slowing topic of illustrations in early newspapers. The labyrinthine opening sentence – which turns helplessly this way and that, like a lost child at the fair – stretches over a spirit-crushing 28 lines before finally spluttering to a halt after no fewer than 176 words. Even then, the merciless sub-editor can't quite find it in his heart to begin a new paragraph, and this turgid essay ploughs on with barely a pause. There were several suicides reported in the days that followed. It's possible at least one of them was a despairing reader of *The Graphic*.

The discouraging design of Victorian newspapers can be explained and forgiven by the limitations of the available technology. But the wayward news sense is rather harder to fathom. It's not as if Victorian Britain was starved of the kind of stories that had what's known in the trade as the 'hey Doris' factor. Death dominated life. Yet incidences of extra-ordinary misfortune, the sort that would now send reporters scrambling to the scene, routinely command a cursory few words. They may be a cursory few words told with a barely-disguised relish for grisly detail, but they're a cursory few words all the same.

Yet with space at a premium, editors still had plenty of col-umn inches to spare for leaden reports of pompous meetings in which little of consequence was discussed or decided. Take the *Lincolnshire Chronicle* of August 21, 1896, for instance. It devotes hundreds and hundreds of words to an update on the visit of the Chinese statesman Li Hongzhang, but the first-ever death in a car accident, which ended the days of the unfortu-nate Mrs Driscoll of Croydon, is brushed aside in a measly four lines at the foot of an athletics report.

All in all, then, you'd be forgiven for thinking that settling down with the average Victorian newspaper is time that could be more usefully spent watching Belgian paint dry. You'd be wrong. Granted, you need to look a little harder to find your reward, but buried beneath the brambles-thick design, smothered by ornate language, gasping for air amid the drab, overblown stories about clerical commissions, royal toasts and suchlike, Victorian news-papers prove a rich seam of hidden history.

There was a time, not very long ago, when you had three main options if you wanted to mine that seam. You could pitch up at the offices of your local newspaper, if it's still there, and ask to be directed to the dustiest corner of their archive, then wrestle manfully with hefty old bound volumes of back-issues. You could sit in your nearest records office, whirring steadily through reels of microfilm. Or you could head to north London.

Colindale Avenue, NW9 is an unlikely sort of spot to find treasure, but for more than 100 years it was home to the British Library's unrivalled collection of British and Irish newspapers.

Here, on a workaday street on the third-to-last stop on the Edgware branch of the Northern Line, 50,000 titles were squirreled away for posterity in nearly 700,000 bound volumes, stretching along 28 miles of shelving. At the time of writing, they're in the process of being shipped off to a new climate-controlled store in Boston Spa, Yorkshire. Why? As with today's papers, print has been upstaged by the internet.

The British Newspaper Archive is a grand project on a scale the Victorians themselves would applaud. Millions of pages from the past are being systematically digitised and uploaded to a rapidly-expanding website. Instead of browsing editions one by one, in the faint hope of stumbling across a reference to – hmmm, let's think – a court report of a bearded woman in an unseemly brawl with a snake-charmer, you can plunge directly in to billions of words of text all at once to see if it ever happened.

For academics and genealogists, it's a godsend. Many books to come will use the archive to shine new light into neglected nooks and crannies of British history and draw perceptive conclusions. This book is not one of them. It is, instead, a collection of thingamajigs and whatnots from journalism's odds and sods drawer. An escaped python in Middlesbrough is stoned to death by boys. A woman lives with her husband's decomposing corpse to keep claiming his pension. A pistol-packing theatre-goer shoots the baddie in a play. A drunken monkey goes berserk in a bar. A man covered in bees moves gingerly through central London. And a bearded lady – yes! – brawls with a snake-charmer. That's our level. Think of this as a tenner plucked from the back of history's sofa, if you wish. Or a fiver, at least.

Are the stories all true? Maybe, but the lack of detail in some articles – names, dates, even places – seems altogether too convenient. Geoffrey Crowther, the editor of *The Economist* from the late 1930s to the mid-1950s, used to tell his journalists to 'simplify and exaggerate'. Some of the ones here may have gone a tad further.

Even if the reporters were playing it perfectly straight, there's always a chance they had got themselves in a horrible muddle. On a Monday in October 1888, a vexed young man strode into London's Dalston Police Court brandishing a weekly newspaper that had announced a disturbing death. The body of George Culley, of 108 Duncombe Road, Upper Holloway, it said, had been found in the shrubs at the Alexandra Palace, with a bottle of laudanum beside him. The news had been particularly startling to the man in court, as he was George Culley, of 108 Duncombe Road, Upper Holloway, and had merely chanced upon the corpse. You may want to bear that in mind as you read on.

True or not, these are the stories that enthralled and appalled their Victorian readers. Some of them are funny. Some are sad; some desperately so. A few of them are bonkers. Virtually all of them are completely forgotten, even in the very places they played out.

If you're an author with writer's block, stuck for a decent plot, they may well prove your salvation. Can I point you to page 38? And 44. Oh and 111 and 144 and 159 …

ANIMALS

~ Preface ~

In his room in a hotel in the sedate Welsh resort of Llandrindod Wells, Mr T.J. Osborne is preparing to check out and head home. It's a June afternoon. The window is open. A fully-grown African lion leaps in.

In the animated few minutes that follow, Mr Osborne gets a crash-course in lion-taming and later becomes the hero of a pithy write-up in the papers. Well, some of them at least. A hotel guest tackling a lion in Llandrindod may seem to us now – as it must have to Mr Osborne then – a remarkable turn of events, but the news editors of the day weren't much impressed.

Perhaps they'd just grown weary of variations on a well-worn theme. In the nineteenth century, ferocious beasts roamed the British countryside once more, thanks to the lax security of travelling shows like Wombwell's Menagerie that criss-crossed the nation in the style of incontinent mice, leaking wherever they went.

In Nottingham, a tiger was found lurking in an orchard. Two elephants cheerfully demolished a back garden in Market Harborough. In Burton, brewery workers at Bass formed a human cordon as an escaped kangaroo bounced through the town, its erstwhile keepers giving wheezy chase. Time and time again in the papers of the era, something alarming is at large in a place nature never intended it to be.

The root cause of all this drama was the Victorians' unquenchable thirst for novelty, which drew exotic creatures from the outposts of the empire to British shores. The UK soon found itself at the centre of a thriving new trade, a livestock exchange that symbolised man's domination of the animal kingdom, Britain's domination of the globe and above all, money's domination of absolutely everything.

If you had £600 to spare in the 1890s, for instance, a man named William Cross could secure you a hippo. He was quite a chap, Mr Cross. Customers from all ranks of society came to his store in Liverpool, reported the *Manchester Weekly Times*, 'from His Royal Highness the Prince of Wales down to the tender-hearted crossing sweeper desirous of having stuffed a favourite sparrow'.

Bewildered animals by their thousands were shipped to his shop to meet the demand. 'About 80,000 parrots pass through my hands every year', he told the paper, adding that he took up to 500 monkeys in one go, flogging off the common Indian ones to organ grinders at 7s 6d a piece. Snakes, baboons, tigers, elephants, sea-lions, buffaloes, rhinos, he'd sold the lot. And for two hundred and fifty quid, you could walk away as the proud owner of a lion, and unwittingly liable for any unexpected damage to a Welsh hotel room.

'Bull in a China Shop'

The strange sight of a bull in a china shop was actually witnessed yesterday in Ilford, from whence the animal was being driven in company with a herd.

It rushed into the shop kept by Mr Barnes, and got firmly wedged behind the counter – so firmly indeed that both counter and fittings had to be moved in order to extricate the beast. A large crowd assembled, and several police were required to keep order.

Strange to say, no serious damage was done by the bull, but a great deal of china placed outside the shop was broken by the crowd in their eagerness to see the strange and unwelcome customer within.

The Yorkshire Telegraph and Star, Sheffield, January 19, 1899

An Intoxicated Monkey

An intoxicated monkey caused a lively scene at Reilly's Hotel, at Coney Island, New York, on Thursday. The monkey is kept in the bar, and is prevented from escaping by a long chain fastened round its waist.

A visitor treated the beast to four cocktails, which made it drunk and bad tempered. It wanted more cocktails, and, being refused, seized a whisky bottle, and, striking the visitor on the head with it, sent him senseless to the floor.

The bar tender tried to seize the animal, but it repulsed him by a blow with another bottle, which broke and cut his head.

The monkey then stood at the back of the bar and pelted everyone with bottles and glasses, several persons being wounded.

The proprietor tried to quiet the beast, but received a bottle of Vermouth in the face, and had some of his front teeth knocked out. The monkey smashed all the mirrors and every bottle of liquor it could reach. The police were at last sent for and lassoed it.

The Manchester Evening News, September 2, 1899

Extraordinary and Startling Appearance of a Runaway Horse at a Tea-Party, at Wragby, Lincolnshire

A scene occurred on Saturday last at Wragby, which we shall find it difficult to describe by mere words; we must, therefore, refer our readers to the front page of this week's *Police News*. The large engraving gives a faithful representation of the consternation caused by an unlooked-for visitor to a family tea-party.

The particulars of this remarkable and singular freak of an animal of the genus equine are as follows. It appears that the driver of the mail cart between Horncastle and Langworth, Lincolnshire, was performing his usual journey Saturday last; the horse he was driving had always been accounted a steady going, docile animal, being, as horsedealers say, 'warranted free from vice.'

After proceeding along for some considerable distance without any mishap, one of the traces broke and the mail cart-horse all of a sudden dashed off at a furious rate. He, luckily

EXTRAORDINARY AND STARTLING APPEARANCE OF A RUNAWAY HORSE AT A TEA PARTY AT WRAGBY, LINCOLNSHIRE.

for the driver, disengaged himself from the cart after which, like Mazeppa's wild steed, he 'urged on his mad career.' He did not meet with any vehicle on the road, and consequently no fatal or serious accident occurred.

At length upon reaching Wragby the animal bolted through the window of a house occupied by Mr Weightman and landed on a tea-table where ten persons were just taking tea.

The panic-struck family and guests started back, but strange to say no one was hurt, but the crockery and furniture sustained serious damage from the hoofs of the eccentric quadruped, who was not secured until he had broken no end of crockery, and smashed up the furniture. At length the uninvited guest suffered himself to be conducted out of the house.

The Illustrated Police News, March 23, 1867

Elephants On The Loose
A Keeper Killed. Panic At A Concert

A remarkable scene occurred at the Crystal Palace, London, on Sunday afternoon. Two elephants forming part of the circus which closed its season there on Saturday escaped from control, and after killing a keeper invaded the refreshment-room and then ran amok through the transepts.

A concert was in progress and the audience scattered in all directions, a terrible panic being only narrowly averted. Finally the Palace was closed and one elephant captured. The other escaped through the grounds and was caught on Sunday evening at Beckenham.

A later account by a representative of the Press Association who visited the Palace on Sunday night says that one of the elephants who escaped was a large animal known as 'Charlie.'

All the keepers succeeded in getting clear but one who was overtaken just at the door and trampled to death. The other beast made its way across the nave to the buffet and thence to the concert-room.

Much alarm was caused, but the elephant did not attempt to pursue the flying crowd, turning in an opposite direction, proceeding through the glass and wooden framework into the centre transept.

Tearing down some 15 feet of the wall it walked leisurely around, and then proceeded to make its way through numerous side courts and the roller skating rink to the door opening on the North Tower Gardens, by which it made its final exit.

'Charlie' meanwhile quietly stood over one of the numerous statues in the south nave. Cyanide of potassium had, however, to be administered to it before it could be taken into custody. Then it was led back and chained to a younger elephant. Charlie was afterwards shot.

The Western Times, Exeter, February 20, 1900

Peculiar Railway Accident

On Saturday morning a ferocious bull rushed at a train on the Llandilo branch of the North Western Railway, killing itself and throwing two carriages off the line. The passengers escaped with a good shaking, and after being transferred to fresh carriages the train proceeded all right.

The Dundee Courier and Argus, June 14, 1881

———◆———

A Puma in a Schoolroom

A Denver (Colorado) correspondent records a remarkable act of bravery on the part of an 18-year-old girl, a school teacher in the village of Owyhee.

While Eva Bates, the girl in question, was teaching her class an enormous puma, or mountain lion, sprang into the room, and falling upon a little antelope, which had been brought there by a child, whose pet it was, killed it, and at once began to devour it.

The children were panic-stricken, and fled to a corner of the room, where they huddled together for mutual protection, while the puma, which had left the dead antelope, seemed to be preparing to attack them.

As soon as the antelope had fallen the little teacher saw she would have to be prepared to defend her charges, and remembering that there was a gun loaded with small shot in the next room, she decided to get it.

To do this she was compelled to cross the room and go out by the door which opened near where the puma was crouching. She hurried by, and in a moment seized the weapon.

Then she lay flat on the floor, and, creeping along quietly with the gun in front of her, pushed it until the muzzle rested against the head of the beast, and a moment later, as he was about to spring, she drew the trigger, and the beast fell back with its head blown to atoms.

The Whitstable Times and Herne Bay Herald, January 12, 1895

A Swarm of Bees on a Man's Back

Considerable excitement was caused in Oxford Circus, Regent Street and some of the West End thoroughfares the other morning by the appearance of a man whose back, from his collar to his waist, was literally covered with bees, whilst hundreds more hovered over his head and all around him.

The man walked on in a state of evident fear, and as may be imagined this strange sight in the midst of the crowded streets led to his being followed by a large crowd. It seemed that the man was in the employ of Messrs. Mappin and Webb, and was ordered to convey a swarm of bees, which had been enclosed in a basket, to a railway station.

Whilst in the act of placing the basket in a van, the lid came off and the queen bee and her followers, numbering many thousands, swarmed upon the man's back, shoulders and head. Terribly frightened, he made an attempt to run away, but the bees maintained their hold, and the man walked about in the hope that his friends would take their departure. Ultimately, a bystander advised him to throw off his coat. Taking the hint, he slipped off his garment, when the host of bees rose *en masse* and the man made off as quickly as possible, and so did the bystanders. Strange to say, the man was only slightly stung in the neck.

The Whitstable Times and Herne Bay Herald, July 18, 1885

An Extraordinary 'Dog Story'

Considerable interest was excited in Leicester by the publication of a remarkable, and indeed almost incredible, 'dog story' from the accident ward of the local infirmary.

It is related that while a Bible woman was visiting the accident ward some days ago and talking to one of the patients, a terrier dog made its way to her with difficulty from near one of the adjoining beds, and appealingly held up one of its fore paws.

She called the attention of one of the doctors to the animal, and it was then found that the limb was broken. The bones were set and a bed made up for the canine sufferer in the ward, due instructions being entered upon the patient's card as to his treatment and diet.

The animal progressed favourably, and became a general favourite with both the patients and officials, until a day or two ago, when it was claimed by its owner and taken away.

How the terrier found its way to the infirmary is not known, but it entered the institution unobserved, and curiously enough, was found in the accident ward, where men were being treated for ailments similar to that with which the dog was afflicted.

But it will be readily believed that the officials and patients regretted to part with so interesting a patient – one that proved so amenable to treatment and discipline.

The North-Eastern Daily Gazette, Middlesbrough,
March 26, 1896

A Child Stolen by a Monkey

A local paper reports a somewhat remarkable case of purloining a child, which occurred in the small village of Manxbridge, in Somersetshire, on Monday last.

It appears that Mr Judcote, a gentleman of independent means, has for a long time past kept a large monkey, who has been accustomed to range over his master's garden and grounds, as the creature was esteemed harmless, and, to use a sporting phrase, 'was warranted to be free from vice.'

On Monday last, Mrs Hemmingway, near neighbour of Mr Judcote's, while walking in her garden, was surprised and horrified at beholding 'Hulch,' Mr Judcote's monkey, suddenly snatch her baby from the arms of her youngest sister Clara, who, as a special favour, had been permitted to take charge of the infant.

The monkey, gibbering and chattering, rushed off with its prize, and gained the roof of an outhouse with very little difficulty. Mrs Hemmingway was driven to the uttermost extremity of despair, and she vainly strove to repossess herself of her last born.

She beheld, to her infinite horror, the monkey pass over the roof of the outhouse, until he and his burden were both lost to sight. The anxious mother at once hastened to the house of her neighbour, Mr Judcote, who appeared to be as much troubled as herself at the unlooked-for disaster.

His man-servants were despatched in every direction in search of 'Hulch,' who was however, too wary to allow his hiding place to be discovered. In the meantime the parents of the child were kept in a constant state of anxiety and trepidation. It was impossible to say what had befallen the child.

A CHILD STOLEN BY A MONKEY.

The day passed over without any news of either 'Hulch' or the infant, and it was by merest chance that both the fugitives were discovered by some farm labourers in an adjacent wood towards eight o'clock in the evening.

At this time 'Hulch' seemed to be tired of his companion, whom he purposely resigned to the farm servants. The delight of the parents upon regaining their child may be more readily imagined than described.

The Illustrated Police News, July 9, 1870

An Alligator in a Bedroom

A correspondent at Ajmere sends the *Times of India* particulars of a curious adventure with an alligator.

At the sacred city of Pokur, near Ajmere, one of the numerous alligators which abound in the lake there, and which are looked upon with the greatest reverence by the Brahmins, managed to crawl from the water up a flight of high stone steps into the courtyard of a house used by the European officials and visitors as a dak bungalow. It is supposed that the reptile was frightened by some noise.

Turning, it missed the steps which would have led it back to the safety of the water and entered the room in which the servants were sleeping.

The astonishment of the men at finding themselves lashed by the tail of the monster in the dark may be imagined. Their master, coming with a light, found the alligator, which was ten feet long, hard up against the wall on one of the servants' beds.

The Brahmins are highly incensed at this gentleman for shooting the alligator even under these circumstances and have preferred a complaint to the Commissioner of the district.

It is doubtless very necessary to respect the feelings, especially the religious feelings, of our fellow men; but it does seem rather hard to object to one's shooting an alligator when he gets into your servant's bed in the middle of the night.

The Edinburgh Evening News, December 1, 1876

Fight Between a Wolf and a Baboon

A remarkable fight was witnessed at Chicago the other night in the window of a shop occupied by a dealer in animals.

It took place after the premises had been closed for the night. An immense cage filled the window, and contained 'a happy family,' among which were a grey wolf and two baboons.

The wolf snapped at the female baboon, and the male, resenting it, attacked the wolf, which was a large specimen and considerably larger than himself. The battle, which was a desperate one, lasted for half an hour, the wolf giving evidence of being considerably stronger, but the baboon was decidedly cleverer and quicker in his mode of attack.

The fight was, however, a very unequal one, and the monkey got rapidly tired, becoming at last too weak to defend himself from the wolf, which throttled him to death. The female baboon tried to help her mate, but she was too small and weak to be of any service against the superior strength of her antagonist.

The occurrence created a great deal of excitement, and a crowd of fully a thousand people gathered to witness it. Several tried to interfere, and distract the attention of the animals by beating on the window-pane, but could not succeed, and it was impossible to get into the shop.

When the wolf was examined next morning he was found to have been very badly bitten and scratched.

The Whitstable Times and Herne Bay Herald,
January 12, 1895

Fearful Attack on a Steamer by Alligators – Three Seamen Devoured

The *Palatka* (Florida) *Herald* publishes an account of a desperate attack on a river steamer by alligators. The steamer whilst going up the Ocklawaha river, and on rounding Sockett's Point, where the stream widens and deepens, suddenly encountered a sea of alligators, floundering and splashing water in all directions.

The captain of the vessel says he never saw such a scene, and never wishes to do so again. Before the speed of the little vessel could be checked she was in the midst of the monsters. To go back or to go ahead was impossible. The passengers endeavoured to drive them away by shooting, and the hands on board beat them with band-spikes, yet they were determined to obstruct the passage of the boat.

The situation became more critical, and the crew and passengers more and more exhausted, and the destruction of the

FEARFUL ATTACK ON A STEAMER BY ALLIGATORS—SEVERAL SEAMEN DEVOURED

boat seemed inevitable. Already three of the crew had been destroyed and several others wounded. Several of the planks were torn from the hull, and the vessel was with difficulty kept from sinking. Just at this period a source of relief came.

A huge serpent appeared making his way from the lakes, the same, it is supposed, that was seen at 'Devil's Elbow' last year. The alligators soon disappeared, following the sea devil, and such fighting never was witnessed. A point below where the river suddenly narrows, soon became blocked with dead alligators, and the river was red with blood.

It is difficult to account for the number and sudden appearance of these animals, but the latest theory may throw some light upon the subject. It is believed by many that there is a large subterranean passage of water between the head waters of the Ocklawaha and the waters of the Ocklawaha lake, and these monsters have found their way here in great numbers, and if not soon exterminated will obstruct the navigation of the Ocklawaha.

The Illustrated Police News, August 26, 1871

Curious Adventure Near Ilfracombe

An Ilfracombe correspondent states that a party of visitors sailing in a pleasure yacht off Lee yesterday afternoon met with an extraordinary adventure.

A large fish suddenly jumped on board and with its tail smashed all the vessel's gear and broke the main boom. A gentleman received a blow in the face which blacked his eye.

The fish then thrust its nose in the cabin, and remained quiet, and the party made for the shore.

The unwelcome visitor proved to be a whale thrasher, fifteen feet long and weighing half a ton. The fish is now exhibited in Ilfracombe.

The Western Times, Exeter, September 5, 1899

An Elephant's Revenge

Some time ago, Mr Sanger, the proprietor of a circus, dismissed an attendant upon his elephants, a man named Baker, for cruelty to the animals. Last week Baker obtained a fresh engagement from Mr Sanger as labourer.

On Sunday evening, Baker went to the stables to fetch a man, named Tottenham, to his tea, when the elephant Charlie, hearing his voice, rushed at him and pierced his skull with his tusk. The unfortunate man died shortly after he was removed from the stable.

The Western Gazette, Yeovil, January 15, 1897

A Queer Importation.
180,000 Mummified Cats

A Liverpool firm has just received a consignment of nineteen tons of embalmed cats, which are to be used as manure.

The cargo contains no less than 180,000 of the feline species, supposed to have been buried two thousand years before Christ in a subterranean cemetery about two hundred miles from Cairo, into which an Egyptian fellah was accidentally precipitated.

The cats were found laid out in rows, one on the top of the other, and carefully embalmed as though Egyptian mummies. They were bought for consignment in Egypt at 78s 9d per ton.

The Dundee Courier and Argus, February 4, 1890

A Cat Walking Seventy Miles

Some weeks a family named Shaker lived at Dawley, in the County of Salop, but had occasion to leave and come to Nottingham. They of course removed all their 'household goods,' including a fine cat, which had been in the family for years.

Arriving at Nottingham the cat showed signs of dissatisfaction with her new abode, and after a few days disappeared, to return to her old home at Dawley, to the great surprise of the neighbours. As might be expected she was very footsore and lame, but otherwise all right.

The distance travelled on foot by the cat, from Nottingham to Dawley, is over seventy miles. Hundreds have flocked to see the four-footed pedestrian, and large sums have been refused by the owners for their favourite.

The Grantham Journal, April 20, 1878

An Escaped Python at Middlesbrough.
Stoned To Death By Boys.

About nine o'clock this morning considerable consternation was created at the lower end of Gladstone Street, near the bridge at the foot of Boundary Road, Middlesbrough, by the appearance of a snake measuring 12 feet in length.

A large number of boys collected and began stoning the escaped reptile, and succeeded in beating its head to a pulp. When PC Dixon arrived on the scene at half-past nine the python was still alive, and no one dare approach it.

Ultimately the injuries which the reptile had suffered to its head caused its death, and it was taken to Dr Veitch, the hon. Curator of the Middlesbrough Museum, who identified it as an Indian Rock Snake (python malurus), a live example of which species he had killed in order to be stuffed and placed in the Museum.

It is not known how the reptile came to be in the town, but during the past few weeks a sensational performance by Cleopatra, the snake charmer, has been given at the Exhibition in Victoria Square, and it is conjectured that this specimen is one of the snakes used in the performance, as it is of the same size, marking, and description.

Some nine hundredweights of snakes were used by Cleopatra, as the snakes could not be used at every performance, and needed rest. The place where the snake was found is considerably over a quarter of a mile from where the exhibition was held.

The snake's skin is in a good state of preservation, and Mr G.W. Duncan of the Gladstone Hotel, has secured it for £5, which amount goes to the infirmary, and will have it stuffed.

The North-Eastern Daily Gazette, Middlesbrough,
November 3, 1898

SCHOOLBOYS HAVE AN EXCITING EXPERIENCE

Strange Birth

A boy in the district of Kirkcaldy who has a passion for chicken-hatching, got a large egg some time ago from some sailors just come from Alexandria, and placed it under a favourite hen, expecting to get a large Egyptian fowl but his surprise and amazement may be better conceived than described when he found one morning a live crocodile!

The Hampshire Telegraph and Sussex Chronicle, August 25, 1849

Wrecking of a Circus
Alligators and Deadly Snakes at Large

An accident near Altoona, Penn., reported on Friday proves to have been very serious. A special train of 14 cars, containing Main's Circus, while descending a steep grade on a branch of the Pennsylvania Railway was totally wrecked by the breaking of an axle on the front car.

The entire train was thrown down a 35ft slope. Seven men and 49 trained horses were instantly killed. Many of the animals were wounded and had to be shot.

A man-slaying ape – a most dangerous creature – escaped, but was caught, as well as one lion. Another lion escaped; a third was lassoed and tied to a tree. A bear, a hyena, a tiger, and others were confined in a similar manner. Another tiger leaped into a farmyard where a woman was milking and killed the cow; it was shot while eating its victim.

The alligators and some valuable and deadly snakes are scattered about the vicinity.

The Manchester Weekly Times, June 9, 1893

Extraordinary Escape of a Tiger in Ratcliff Highway.
Frightful Attack of the Animal on a Boy

Yesterday, between twelve and one o'clock at noon, the inhabitants of St George's-in-the-East (alias Ratcliff Highway), were suddenly thrown into a state of the utmost alarm in consequence of the escape of a large tiger from the warehouse of Mr Jamrach, the extensive importer of wild beasts, &c., of No. 180, Ratcliff Highway, whereby a boy, named John Wade, aged five years, was very seriously injured, and other parties' lives were placed in great jeopardy.

It appears that yesterday morning Mr Jamrach received several boxes, containing two tigers, a lion, and other animals, from the steam ship Germany, lying off Hambro' Wharf, near the Custom House, Lower Thames Street, City. The packages were safely placed in a van, and conveyed to the warehouse in Betts Street, St George's-in-the-East, followed by a crowd of men, women, and children, where a number of labourers adopted means to unload the vehicle.

They had removed several boxes into the premises in safety, and had just lowered a large iron-bound cage on to the pavement in front of the gateway when Police Constable Stewart requested the persons standing round to keep back in case of an accident.

The next moment the occupant (a fine full-sized tiger) became restless, and forced out one end of the cage, when the spectators rushed in every direction from the spot in a state of extreme terror. The tiger appeared to be in a state of madness, and ran along the pavement in the direction of Ratcliff Highway, where it seized the little boy, John Wade, by the upper part of the right arm.

The enraged animal was followed by Mr Jamrach and his men several yards, when the former obtained possession of a crowbar and struck the tiger upon the head and nose, which caused it to relinquish its hold. In the meanwhile ropes were procured, and the savage beast was secured and dragged into the premises, where it was firmly fastened up by the keepers.

The poor boy was raised up by Stewart, the police officer, in a state of great suffering with two severe lacerated wounds on the arm and right side of the face, and it was quite a miracle he was not torn to pieces. The teeth of the animal passed completely through the right arm.

A cab was procured, in which the wounded boy was conveyed to the London Hospital, where Mr Forbes, the house surgeon, rendered every assistance. The boy was in a very low state from loss of blood from the wounds, and last evening, at seven o'clock, he was in a very precarious condition, both from the injuries and shock to the system through fright.

At the time of the escape of the animal the tradespeople in the neighbourhood closed their shops, and remained in a state of fear and anxiety for nearly half an hour afterwards.

It seems that Mr Jamrach is an extensive importer and exporter of all kinds of wild beasts and foreign birds, which he forwards to all parts of the world for menageries and private collections.

The Standard, London, October 27, 1857

Extraordinary Fight

Our readers doubtless noticed, a few days back, an account of a tiger which escaped from a cattle truck in Ratcliff Highway, London, and which, after running along the centre of the road for some distance, was caught by his keepers while in the act of tearing a lad who unfortunately crossed the animal's path.

The tiger was the property of Mr Jamrach, and he sold

it a day or two afterwards to Mr Edmonds, the successor of Wombwell, for his well-known travelling menagerie, which it joined on Monday at West Bromwich. It was placed in one of the ordinary carriages, of two compartments, the adjoining den being occupied by a very fine lion, six or seven years old, for which Mr Edmonds gave £300 three years ago.

The attendants had all left the menagerie to go to breakfast, when suddenly those in the carriage which the proprietors occupy were alarmed by an unusual outcry among the beasts. They soon discovered the cause. The newly-bought tiger had burglariously broken through the 'slide' or partition dividing his den from that of the lion, and had the latter in his terrible grasp.

The combat which ensued was a terrific one. The lion acted chiefly on the defensive, and having probably been considerably tamed by his three years' confinement the tiger had the advantage. His attacks were of the most ferocious kind. The lion's mane saved his head and neck from being much injured, but the savage assailant at last succeeded in ripping up his belly, and then the poor animal was at the tiger's mercy. The lion was dead in a few minutes.

The scene was a fearful one. The inmates of every den seemed to be excited by the conflict, and their roaring and howling might have been heard a quarter of a mile distant. Of course Mr Edmonds and his men could not interfere while the conflict lasted, but when the tiger's fury had subsided they managed to remove the carcase.

He must have used his paws as a sort of battering ram against the partition, as it was pushed in rather than torn down. He cost Mr Edmonds £400.

The Isle of Wight Observer, November 14, 1857

A Civil Crocodile

Some six weeks ago a lively young crocodile contrived, one night, to effect its escape from Josepha Choikowa's travelling menagerie, then exhibiting at Kuschwarda [in Bohemia], and all the efforts made to discover its hiding-place in the neighbouring brooks and ponds proving fruitless, its proprietress, after three days' search gave it up as irretrievably lost, and departed on her further professional rounds.

A month later the smith of Salsau, a village not far from Kuschwarda, was strolling home towards evening through the rain, when he suddenly espied, lying in a huge puddle on the high road, what he took to be a drunken man, prostrate and helpless.

Upon wading into the mud, with the charitable intention of extricating the recumbent one from so miry a bed, he perceived to his astonishment that the object of his solicitude was the missing crocodile. Nothing daunted, he fastened a rope round the saurian's scaly body behind its shoulders, and led it along until he met a cart, into which, with the assistance of the driver, he managed to lift it.

The crocodile made no resistance, but followed its captor as meekly as though it had been a tame dog tied to a string. On subsequent examination it was found to have increased in size and weight during its spell of liberty, and to be, for a crocodile, in excellent health and spirits.

What it was fed upon while roaming about the country, and how it had kept out of the cold during the chilly nights of May and June, are still mysteries to its owner, who has joyfully recovered possession of her truant.

The Illustrated Police News, July 24, 1880

A Monkey's Suicide

At Goldsboro, N.C. the other day, occurred one of the most novel suicides of the century, the victim being a monkey owned by Mr Rockwell Syrock.

The animal was quite a favourite with all the children for miles around and knew most of them. For several years, Jocko's owner had been in the habit of visiting all the hangings in this portion of the state, taking the mischievous animal with him.

A MONKEY'S SUICIDE

The monkey always seemed to take an especial interest in such horrible proceedings.

On the 25th June, Alexander Howard was to have been executed for the murder of an old man, but the Governor respited him. The gibbet made for carrying out the sentence had been erected before the executive interposed his power and postponed it. Syrock visited the gaol with the monkey and examined these preparations.

The animal seemed to be unusually curious and watched the scaffold and trap with earnest eyes. Since that time he has been playing hanging in his master's barn. One morning he was found dead, suspended by a clothes line to one of the rafters of the building.

The Illustrated Police News, August 7, 1880

Elephant in Possession.
A Joyous Interloper

On Thursday considerable commotion was created in the neighbourhood of Lake Road, Landport, by an extraordinary escapade of the elephant 'Picaninny,' belonging to Mr Dan Sullivan, the 'strong man' now performing at the People's Hall of Varieties in that thoroughfare.

The animal, which was stabled in a store behind some premises in Clarendon Street, belonging to Mr F. Pearce, the proprietor of the hall, escaped from the building by breaking open the door and having found its way into an adjoining alley, abutting Timpson Street, entered the house of a man named

Charles Tubbs, where it remained unobserved for a considerable time.

Both Mr and Mrs Tubbs happened to be away from home when the animal gained admission by forcing open the front door. Finding no one to interfere with its diversions, it proceeded to demolish the contents of the two rooms on the ground floor.

Meanwhile its escape from the stable was discovered by the keeper, who, on going to the place for the purpose of feeding his 'little pet,' was dismayed to find the store unoccupied. A thorough search of the premises was followed by an inspection of the open ground adjoining, but no trace of the missing animal could be discovered, and the owner ultimately offered a reward of £1 to anyone who could give him information as to its whereabouts.

Presently Mr Tubbs returned home, and noticed that some turf in front of his cottage had been torn up. This he attributed to mischievous boys, but on reaching the door he observed that the window blind downstairs had disappeared, and at the same moment heard a peculiar noise, apparently proceeding from the back of the premises.

Peering through a back window, he was astonished to find the apartment tenanted by Picaninny, of whose escape he had heard. The animal was playfully throwing some pictures about the room with its trunk.

The keeper was soon brought upon the scene, and with some trouble the elephant was coaxed through the narrow passage, and led out of the house to safe quarters. Mr Tubbs has been satisfactorily compensated from the damage.

The Evening News, Portsmouth, October 14, 1892

John Lubbock's Pet Wasp

Perhaps the strangest pet ever kept by man was a wasp which Sir John Lubbock caught in the Pyrenees and resolved to tame.

He began by teaching it to take its meals on his hand, and although the tiny creature was at first shy of going through its *table d'hôte* on such an unusual festive board, in a very short space of time it grew to expect to be fed in that way.

Sir John preserved this pet with the greatest care. True, it stung him once, but then it had every excuse for doing so. Sir John was examining it on a railway journey, and, the door being opened by a ticket collector, he unceremoniously stuffed it into a bottle, and the outraged Spaniard, not feeling quite at home during the process, gave him a gentle reminder as to the proper way to treat a guest.

The wasp was a pet in every sense of the word, and became so fond of its owner that it allowed itself to be stroked.

It enjoyed civilisation for just nine months, when it fell ill, and although Sir John did all he could to prolong its life, it died.

Many wasps have been under Sir John's observation, but he has never had such a genuine pet as this one.

The Sunderland Daily Echo and Shipping Gazette,
March 16, 1899

A Lion Loose

Mr T.J. Osborne of Old Market Street, Neath, was the subject of a strange adventure at the Bridge Hotel, Llandrindod Wells, on Friday afternoon, about half-past three o'clock. Mr Osborne was preparing to leave for home by the afternoon train on that day, when a full-grown African lion dashed in through the open window. Mr Osborne seized a chair to defend himself. At this instant the lion's keeper and a staff of men appeared on the scene. The keeper warned Mr Osborne not to stir. With as little delay as possible the keeper and his assistants made their way to the room with the necessary appliances for recapturing the brute. With some difficulty they succeeded in throwing a sack over the lion's head, after which he was firmly secured with ropes. It was found that the lion had made its escape from Wombwell's menagerie, which was located on a plot of ground near the Bridge Hotel.

Berrow's Worcester Journal, July 6, 1889

A Monkey Murderer and Suicide

An extraordinary occurrence is reported as having happened at Jump, near Barnsley, on Saturday afternoon, and on inquiry the following facts were well authenticated: A miner named John Hines possessed three monkeys, an old one and two young ones, and like the generality of the tribe, the elder one was fond of imitating what was going on in the household.

On Saturday afternoon whilst shaving himself, Hines was called out into the back yard to see after some pigs that had broken out of the sty, and half-shaved as he was he rushed out, leaving the razor on the table, and his pets, apparently oblivious of his movements.

No sooner, however, was his back turned than the father of the two young monkeys seized the razor and commenced to try his 'prentice hand on his offspring. He evidently miscalculated the keenness of the edge, for in the twinkling of an eye he had severed the heads of the little things almost completely from their bodies.

Even here his experiment did not stop, for he next turned the blade against himself with an almost similar result, for he inflicted a deep gash in the throat.

On Hines' return in a few minutes he found his two young pets quite dead, and the father gasping for breath on the ground, bleeding profusely. The author of the mischief lingered until Sunday, and then he too succumbed to his self-inflicted injuries. The affair has excited considerable interest. It is the intention of the owner to have the dead monkeys stuffed.

The Royal Cornwall Gazette, March 20, 1890

⤻ LOVE, MARRIAGE ⤵
and FAMILY

~ *Preface* ~

It was a wedding night to forget for Henry and Mary Glanister of Liverpool. At least, it would have been if they could remember it in the first place.

On the morning of their first day of married life, they woke up apart. The groom had been arrested the evening before and spent the night in a police cell. His new bride would have been furious with him if she hadn't been locked up too.

Perhaps she reserved her rage for her mother instead. After all, Mum started it, according to the *Manchester Evening News* on July 11, 1882, becoming 'so overcome with emotion and liquor that she became uproarious and fell into the hands of the police'. The newlyweds piled in to free her, and ended up behind bars that night rather than in each other's arms.

In that, they weren't unique. Two years later another couple from Liverpool spent their first night as man and wife in the cells. Thomas and Mary McNamara had enjoyed the convivial company of their sisters, cousins and aunts during the afternoon, reported the *Manchester Courier and Lancashire General Advertiser* of October 9, 1884. The drink flowed freely, and when they staggered off to the pub, the barman refused to serve them. 'This by no means pleased the wedding guests', the paper noted, drily. When the police arrived to turf them out, Mrs McNamara punched PC 829 in the face, and it was off to the bridewell for the unsteady bride and groom.

A similar tale of drunken nuptial woe played out in London in October 1868, according to the zippily-titled *Bucks Herald, Uxbridge Advertiser, Windsor and Eton Journal*. Elizabeth Stanton, of Holborn, was dancing in her local when things – in a frustratingly unspecified way – got a little out of hand, and she was asked to leave. By way of reply, she smashed a window, punched the barman then tried to bite a policeman. Twice. You can guess the rest.

These stories, and a few more in the chapter that follows, put a bit of a dent in the theory of French physician Eugene Becklard that marriage is 'the principal medium through which nature makes the human species tranquil and happy'.

Not just that. It also 'purifies the complexion, removes blotches from the skin, invigorates the muscles, makes the carriage erect and free and the voice full and firm'.

These bold claims came in his 1840s work, *Physiological Mysteries and Revelations in Love, Courtship and Marriage: An Infallible Guide-Book for Married and Single Persons, in Matters of Utmost Importance to the Human Race*. Think of it as sex tips for Victorians.

The breed must be crossed, that was his maxim. A melancholy man should pair up with a sprightly woman, and vice versa. The ambitious should unite with the humble. The amiable with the choleric. That way, the danger was minimised of growing bored of each other's company (although you had less chance to grow tired: the mortality rate meant few marriages lasted more than 30 years).

M. Becklard's match-making advice didn't stop with pairing chalk-and-cheese personalities. 'The length of the neck should be proportionably less in the male than the female', he cautioned. The back of the woman should be more hollow than of man; woman should have loins more extended than man … and on he went.

Not everyone needed to pay heed to his fussy strictures. Marriage was a cornerstone of Victorian life, but it wasn't universal. According to the Registrar-General, there were getting on for 1¼ million women aged between 20 and 40 who were unmarried in 1851. Out of 100 women aged 20 and over, 30 were classified as spinsters.

The reasons were nuanced, but ultimately mathematical: women outnumbered men. It certainly didn't help that a rigid class structure limited the choice still further, and that men had a found a taste for emigrating.

Some couples simply couldn't be bothered with getting hitched. In the mid-nineteenth century the journalist Henry Mayhew's survey of working-class London drew him into the world of the costermongers. Only one in ten of the couples living together were married, he found. 'Of the rights of "legitimate" or "illegitimate" children the costermongers

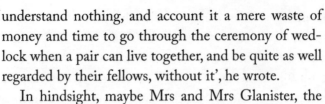

understand nothing, and account it a mere waste of money and time to go through the ceremony of wedlock when a pair can live together, and be quite as well regarded by their fellows, without it', he wrote.

In hindsight, maybe Mrs and Mrs Glanister, the McNamaras and the bellicose Elizabeth Stanton would have agreed.

Extraordinary Duel.
A Strange Test of Bravery

A tarantula is a large insect of the spider tribe, and its bite is as deadly as that of a rattlesnake. The details of a remarkable duel which recently occurred at Las Vegas show the horror with which this terrible spider is regarded in South America.

Two young men – an American and a Mexican – fell out over a young woman they both loved, and the result was that the enmity became too great to be carried, and it was determined to end it in a duel.

The matter came about in an unusual way, however, and it was not a regular challenge and acceptance, but while in company of mutual friends the Mexican taunted the American with being a member of a race of cowards, and said the Americans had no bravery.

The American, of course, disputed this and said he would test the Mexican's bravery if he wished it. He would be willing to go into a dark room with the Mexican and there decide the point. But the stipulation was that in the dark room there should also be a lot of tarantulas turned loose.

If either of them came out alive he was to have the girl. If either showed the white feather and came out before the death of the other or before all the tarantulas were killed he should give up all claim to the girl. The Mexican was disposed to refuse, but the fear of being looked upon as a coward caused him to accept.

The room was prepared, and the two men went in. There were at least a dozen tarantulas in the room and also two scorpions. The American walked boldly into the room and took his stand, while the Mexican followed, but was hesitating in his manner.

The doors had been closed but a short time when the Mexican was heard to scream out that he was bitten and was dying. The doors were opened and he staggered out and fell to the floor. The American walked out unhurt, and then it was found that the Mexican had not been bitten at all, but had scratched his hand on a protruding nail in the wall and had thought it a spider's bite.

The Western Mail, Cardiff, July 15, 1892

Lively Scene at a St Helens Wedding

An extraordinary scene in opposition to a wedding took place in the neighbourhood of Eccleston Street, St Helens, on Monday.

A middle-aged man, who follows the occupation of a coal-hawker, had decided to re-marry, but the new alliance did not meet with the approval of his children.

The man had been a widower but a few weeks, and seeing the 'gathering storm' he went away quietly in the morning, and the ceremony was performed in a church on the outskirts of the borough. Meanwhile preparations were being made for his reception at home.

On returning from church the couple were received by a crowd of people, who laughed and jeered, and evidently intended to show their feelings in an unorthodox fashion. Street sweepings were seized as a substitute for rice, and were thrown upon the couple, and rotten eggs were brought into requisition.

One young fellow struck the bridegroom a blow in the face, which disfigured him, while a young woman seized the bonnet of the bride and tore it up. The bride and bridegroom eventually got inside their house, and remained there. Meanwhile the uproar in the street continued until a late hour.

Charles Houghton, a brother of the bridegroom, was arrested on a charge of being drunk and disorderly. He was brought before Mr Biram and Mr W. Lee Pilkington at the Police Court on Tuesday. Chief Constable Wood stated that the man had been 88 times convicted. He was fined 7s 6d and costs, or 10 days.

Supplement to the Manchester Courier, September 20, 1890

A Female Husband

A coroner's inquest was held on Monday night at Belfast, on the body of a person who for many years has been known as

John Coulter, but who on dying on Sunday from the results of injuries accidentally received was discovered to be a female.

Evidence was given to the effect that for twelve years she had worked in male attire as a labourer at Belfast quays; that 20 years ago she got married in Dungannon to a woman who was examined at the inquest, and deposed that the deceased was her husband; that they had been separated for the past six years on account of the drinking habits of the deceased, whom she throughout described as her husband.

At the time of their marriage the deceased was a farm servant in the employment of her father. The evidence went to show that, as far as could be traced, the deceased had always worn male attire, and had been engaged in work peculiar to men.

The death was the result of injuries sustained by falling downstairs on Sunday last while in a state of intoxication. The woman who had been married to the deceased undertook to inter the remains of her so-called husband.

The York Herald, January 26, 1884

Selling a Wife by Auction

It is only a few months since that a paragraph went the round of the papers relating how a certain stonemason at Rawtenstall, in Rossendale, sold his wife to another man for the sum of £10; but it would seem from certain proceedings which took place last week at Stacksteads, a Rossendale village, that the money value of wives has sadly declined since that event.

A navvy, living at Tunstead Mill, Stacksteads, determined to get rid of the 'partner of his joys and sorrows' by offering her for sale by auction, the highest bidder as usual to take 'the lot.'

On Tuesday last the sale took place at the husband's house, but, despite Solomon's testimony as to a woman being more precious than rubies, and notwithstanding that the spectators were numerous, the highest offer was only 4d, at which low figure the wife was eventually 'knocked down' to another navvy, who, by-the-by, lived next door.

The seller wanted to 'throw in' three children, but the buyer objected, and the bairns were left on hand. The wife, however, went joyfully to the home of her new owner, and seemed to be quite as glad to get away from her late liege lord as he was to part with her.

The occurrence has caused quite a stir in the locality, and has been commented upon by the local press.

The Sheffield and Rotherham Independent, July 29, 1879

Chained to a Bed for Forty Years

An extraordinary case of sequestration has just been disclosed before the Court of Assizes of the Manche, a man having been kept concealed, chained to a bed for a period of forty years, by his own father first, and by a brother afterwards.

In the year 1830 a farmer named Boullaud lived with his wife and four sons – Charles, Jacques, François, and Julien – in the commune of Bomagny. Julien, who was then twenty-two years of age, had shown some signs of a deranged mind, the result of fright while walking out at night, and the father, to escape the trouble of guarding the young man, had him chained by the two wrists on a bed, from which the son was never moved.

The result of the captivity was that Julien's limbs were at length completely paralysed from inaction, and he became a perfect idiot. The father died in 1852, having previously shared his fortune between the three other sons, on condition that Charles and François should each pay a sum of two hundred francs annually for the wants of their brother, while Jacques was to board and lodge him.

CHAINED UP FOR FORTY YEARS

The unfortunate man continued chained to his bed until 1864, when, as he could no longer make any movement, the shackles were taken from him, but it was not till the present year that the facts came to the ears of the judicial authorities. A descent was made at the house, and Julien, now over sixty years of age, was found lying almost naked, and in a miserable condition, on a litter of straw, placed in a dark hole for concealment.

Jacques Boullaud, being arrested, was now brought up for trial, and pleaded in his defence, that he had only continued a state of things commenced by his father. The jury returned a verdict of not guilty, and he was set at liberty.

The Illustrated Police News, July 9, 1870

An Unfortunate Man Who Unwittingly Went In For Bigamy

The strange case of Hiram Macdermott came before the Old Bailey on Monday. Discovering that his wife had a husband living, Macdermott imagined himself free again, and becoming tired of Mrs Macdermott No. 1, quickly replaced her with a sprightlier spouse.

Then it came out that his first wife's previous marriage was itself a bigamous one, and that he Hiram, was now a bigamist himself! Mrs Macdermott No. 2, when she heard all this, promptly gave her husband up to the police, and charged him with bigamy. The prisoner pleaded guilty, and he had to serve six weeks' hard labour.

The Leeds Times, February 18, 1893

A Ludicrous Romance

A tragic-comic romance lately occurred at Budapest. A stripling of seventeen fell in love with a girl three years his junior, and these children were in such despair at the prospect of having to wait so long before they could be married that they decided to commit suicide.

Their last meeting was behind the Custom House. Tears were shed on either side, and some kissing and hugging were gone through. The juvenile couple then repaired to the Danube, and with a fortitude worthy of a better cause the young lady jumped in.

Fortunately she could swim, and availed herself fully of her capabilities in that art. She shrieked for help, which was soon at hand.

Just as she was safely landed her lover fired three revolver shots against himself, but none of them took effect; and a quarter of an hour later the young folks were handed over to their respective parents.

The Tamworth Herald, December 22, 1888

Romantic Story of a Hermit's Life

A telegram from Madrid states that a man has just been discovered who for several years has lived alone in the wild and deserted mountains of Cape de Gata, situated in the southeastern extreme of Spain.

Some years ago he was employed in a factory at Lugo, in Galicia, which is at the opposite end of the country to Cape de Gata.

Becoming enamoured of his employer's daughter, the passion was reciprocated, but the lady's parents had a rich suitor in view, and the factory-worker was discharged. Subsequently the couple eloped, but were overtaken, and when, a few months later, the disconsolate lover ventured to return to Lugo, the lady had married her parents' choice. In his despair he resolved to leave the country, and set sail for Algeria.

The vessel was, however, wrecked, and he was tossed by the waves on to the shore of the desolate Cape de Gata. Here he has remained ever since, and when seen a few days ago by a hunter who had ventured into the country, he presented a savage-like appearance in his covering of wild animals' skins, and with hair and beard grown to an extra-ordinary length. All efforts to induce him to return to civilisation were futile.

The Midland Daily Telegraph, Coventry, September 9, 1892

A Remarkable Story.
A Widow Married To Her Own Brother

From the *Detroit Free Press*: There passed through this city yesterday *en route* to Chicago, a lady whose history is one of the most remarkable ever brought to public notice.

In 1838 her parents emigrated to this country from England, leaving behind them an only son some ten years of age, who had engaged as a cabin boy in a merchant vessel in the East India trade, they landing in New York, when, a few months later, the subject of this sketch was born.

While she was yet a helpless infant, both her parents died,

and she was sent to the Foundling's Home, where she remained some time, when she was finally adopted by a lady and gentleman, who then resided in Elmira, N.Y.

Of course she knew nothing of her sailor brother, and she grew up in the belief that she was really the child of her foster parents. At the age of eighteen she married an industrious young mechanic, and set out for the great West.

After travelling in various states, they finally settled in Missouri, where they continued prosperous and happy until the storm of war burst upon the country.

Then her husband, in common with the thousands of his misguided countrymen, enlisted in the service of the rebellion, and was assigned to General Price's army. He served faithfully during the first eighteen months of the war, but was finally killed in one of the South-western engagements.

From the breaking out of the war the lady of whom we write had lost all trace of her foster parents, owing to the disturbed condition of that portion of the country in which she resided, and after her husband's death she removed to St Louis, where she sought to maintain herself by serving.

In 1863 she again married, and her husband embarked in business in St Louis. This marriage was a thoroughly happy one, and in the course of time two children were born unto them.

The husband gradually extended his business operations, so that much of his time was necessarily spent in travelling about the country, and during one of his business tours he visited Chicago, where he became acquainted with a lady and gentleman, who by a fortunate chain of circumstances, he ascertained were the long lost foster parents of his wife.

Delighted at the discovery he had made, and pleased no doubt with anticipations of the joyful surprise he should give his wife, the husband at once concluded his business with the intention of returning to St Louis and bringing her to Chicago for the purpose of reuniting her with her friends, without having first prepared either party for such an event.

On the night of his contemplated departure for home, while conversing with Mr and Mrs —, it happened that he was led into a recital of his adventures about the world, and before his narrative was finished his listeners knew that their adopted daughter had married her own brother, who, before she was born, had sailed for the East Indies.

Horrified beyond expression, the wretched man fled from the house, and from that hour no tidings of him have ever reached his friends. This was in March last, and a few weeks later the wretched sister-wife was rendered comparatively poor by the destruction by fire of a large portion of the property left in her hands.

Although written to by her stricken friends, their letters never reached her, and a few weeks since she started for Elmira, her native home. Upon her arrival here she learned the address of her foster parents, with whom she at once communicated, giving them full details of her experience since she had first bade them farewell, upon setting out for her Western home.

Their answer to her letter contained a statement of the terrible discovery of the identity of her husband and brother, together with an affectionate invitation to come to them with her children and share their home.

Heart broken, and nearly crazed by the strange *denouement* of her happy married life, the wretched woman hastened to accept the offer, and this morning will doubtless see her re-united to her earliest and dearest friends.

The Dundee Courier and Argus, December 10, 1868

The Baby and its Endowment

The stationmaster at Preesgweene, near Oswestry, received on Tuesday a box containing a live baby and a letter requesting him to adopt it. He declined, and handed the baby with the box and contents over to a signalman, who took the little thing home. On looking over the box he found, besides wearing apparel, £200 in bank-notes. The signalman has now been asked to surrender the baby, but he declines.

The Illustrated Police News, May 5, 1894

An Extraordinary Marriage Ceremony

A few days ago the report of a singular, and we may add melancholy, wedding reached us from Florida, the sum and substance of which is as follows: It would appear from the account furnished us that a Mormon gentleman, named Bradley, left the City of Utah, and after travelling from place to place with samples of his goods he made the acquaintance of a young lady.

The acquaintance it would seem ripened into friendship, and finally a still more tender feeling sprang up in the breasts of both Mr Bradley and his fair enslaver. The gentleman proposed and the lady accepted him, although it was known that she was in the last stage of consumption.

Upon reaching Florida arrangements were made for a speedy union, but the bride elect became so weak and prostrate that she could not venture to move out of the house, and there was some idea of having the ceremony performed in her sick chamber, but this was overruled by his parents before it could be solemnised, and the ill-fated young woman breathed her last, and now comes the most remarkable, and what has been, with justice, termed the most unpleasant and discreditable part of the tale.

The coffin containing the dead body of the young woman was taken into the church, and several young ladies habited as bridesmaids surrounded it, while the clergyman read the marriage service, and then proceeded with the funeral service.

It was stated that Mr Bradley had given his spiritual wife his solemn promise that her body should not be consigned to its last resting place until this objectionable formula had been gone through.

The Illustrated Police News, September 17, 1881

A Young Lady in Ticklish Circumstances

An uproarious scene has occurred at Worksop. On Sunday evening a tradesman escorted to his home and introduced to his wife a young lady, to whom he paid the most marked attention.

The wife protested against her husband's conduct; a row ensued, and the assistance of neighbours was invoked. This only made matters worse, and the husband, to extricate himself from his difficulty, knocked his wife down, and, presenting a pistol at her, threatened to shoot her.

A crowd quickly gathered about the house, and the husband was threatened with summary punishment. He, however, escaped, and the injured wife went and procured a warrant for his apprehension.

On Monday, a large crowd assembled near the house, and with pots and kettles created a most unseemly disturbance. It was not to be supposed that a young lady who could act the part already described would be discomposed by the noisy indignation of a street crowd, and to show that she did not care she made her appearance at the window, and then proceeded up stairs and sat down at the piano.

The crowd thought it improper that such coolness should not be further tested, so a party proceeded up stairs and brought her down into the yard amid the snow. Here she was greeted with loud yells, and a volley of snowballs fell thick and fast upon her.

She succeeded in escaping from the yard, but was closely followed by her tormentors. A friendly door was opened to her, where she found refuge. When it was dark she quietly left the town by train.

The Dundee Courier and Argus, January 5, 1867

A Jealous Woman's Revenge.
Ludicrous Scene.

A most remarkable case of jealousy and revenge reaches us from Blythe. It appears that a young man named Walkingshaw, who is connected with a large London firm who make mantles, skirts, bodices, and other articles of female attire for the trade, paid marked attention to a Miss Bradley, the well-known teacher in a first-class establishment in their neighbourhood.

For some reason or another the Mantelini in the case treated his quondam enslaver with coldness and neglect, and eventually turned her off for another and newer flame. Miss Bradley was a prey to the 'Green-eyed monster.' The demon of jealousy raged in her breast.

On Saturday night last she chanced to meet the 'gay Lothario' with her rival on his arm. Her head seemed to swim, she breathed with difficulty, but contrived to follow the loving pair at a respectful distance.

A turning in the road, however, for a brief period concealed them from her sight. Nevertheless she followed on. Presently she observed young Walkingshaw enter one of the houses in an adjacent street. The people who rented the house in question were well known to her.

She entered, and followed her quondam lover upstairs. In the corner of the passage was a regulation rifle; Miss Bradley seized hold of this as a host of contending passions raged within her breast. Walkingshaw, unconscious of her presence, entered one of the apartments on the second storey.

Miss Bradley, rifle in hand, burst open the door, and beheld her cruel lover's arms round the waist of what she supposed was her rival. She raised the gun to her shoulders, levelled the piece at the hateful object before her, and fired. When the smoke cleared away the real facts were but too apparent.

No mischief was done; the gun was loaded with blank cartridge only; and so far from embracing her rival before her very eyes, Mr Walkingshaw was but trying the effect of a shawl on a dummy made of wood, canvas, and tow. How matters have been arranged we cannot at present say, but rumour says the case will engage the attention of the gentlemen of the long robe.

The Illustrated Police News, November 9, 1872

A JEALOUS WOMAN'S REVENGE!

Married By a Dying Man

An extraordinary phonograph story comes from America. It is said that a Protestant clergyman was very anxious to perform the marriage ceremony for his daughter, but shortly before the day fixed for her wedding he became dangerously ill, and his recovery was pronounced hopeless.

Under these circumstances the dying man ordered a phonograph to be brought to his bedside, and spoke into the instrument his part of the Marriage Service. The phonograph was placed on the Communion table of the church in which the daughter was married to a young merchant of Louisiana, and this voice from the grave, as it were, united the young couple.

The Sunderland Daily Echo and Shipping Gazette, September 5, 1900

Remarkable Fatality.
Five Husbands Meet With Violent Deaths

A remarkable case of fatality attaching to the many successive husbands of one woman is reported from Nevers. A man named Chandiour has just hanged himself in the locality. The circumstances of the suicide are in no way extraordinary, except for the fact that the man was the fifth husband of a woman, all of whose previous husbands came to a violent end.

The first hanged himself, the second perished in a fire, the third drowned himself and the fourth and fifth have both been found hanged, and in each case, strange enough, on a pear tree.

The Western Gazette, Yeovil, January 18, 1901

Kissing In Public Strictly Prohibited

A sensation has just been caused in the States by order issued by the Baltimore Park Board against love-making in the park. General J.S. Berry, secretary of the board, has declared that public parks are not meant as courting-places, and that in the future anything in the way of love-making will be held to be improper conduct and punishable by the police.

Two young people have, in fact, been arrested for kissing, and fined – the man twenty dollars, the woman five dollars: a curious distinction in the value of a kiss.

The order and the decision have caused considerable stir in New York, and the commissioners of the Central Park have been inundated with letters protesting against the Baltimore precedent being followed.

The Citizen, Gloucester, June 10, 1893

Sold His Wife for a Shilling

In Upper Heiduk, in Silesia, a working man recently, so a German paper reports, sold his wife for a term of two years to an acquaintance for a shilling. The wife lived with her new partner in harmony, when one day, the lawful husband thinking he had surrendered her too cheaply, called upon the man and demanded a further sum of 15s. The lady, he said, had a set of beautiful teeth. He had forgotten that, and he considered 15s a small sum under the circumstances.

The 'man in possession' demurred, and the husband sought the aid of the law. The authorities, it appears, pronounced that as he had contracted himself out of his legal rights for two years, and for a 1s, he was not entitled to any further amount.

The Worcestershire Chronicle, May 17, 1890

Glass Eye as a Plea for Divorce

A judge in Ohio has given a decision of peculiar interest to young women. A man sued for divorce on the ground that his wife had a glass eye which she skilfully concealed during courtship by the use of glasses.

The judge refused to grant a divorce, holding that it is not necessary for a woman during her courtship to inform the intended husband of any device or attachment used to improve the work of nature in the construction of the face, form, or figure.

He holds that a glass eye is no more fraudulent than false teeth or hair.

The Leeds Times, April 1, 1899

Her Husband Tickling Her Feet

On Thursday last week, a very serious charge was preferred against a man named Michael Puckridge, who resides at

Winbush, a small village in Northumberland. The circumstances, as detailed before the board of guardians, are of a harrowing nature.

It appears that Puckridge has lived very unhappily with his wife, whose life he has threatened on more than one occasion. Most probably he had long contemplated the wicked design which he carried out but too successfully about a fortnight since.

Mrs Puckridge, who is an interesting looking young woman, has for a long time past suffered from varicose veins in the legs. Her husband told her that he possessed an infallible remedy for this ailment.

TICKLEING A WOMAN'S FEET - A WIFE DRIVEN MAD

She was induced by her tormentor to allow herself to be tied to a plank, which he placed across two chairs. When the poor woman was bound and helpless, Puckridge deliberately and persistently tickled the soles of her feet with a feather.

For a long time he continued to operate upon his unhappy victim, who was rendered frantic by the process. Eventually she swooned, whereupon her husband released her. It soon became but too manifest that the light of reason had fled.

Mrs Puckridge was taken to the workhouse, where she was placed with the insane patients. A little girl who lived in the house, niece of the ill-used woman, spoke to one or two of the neighbours, saying her aunt had been tied to a plank, and that her uncle, so she believed, had cruelly ill-treated her.

An inquiry was instituted, and there is every reason to believe that Mrs Puckridge had been driven out of her mind in the way already described. But the result of the investigation is not yet known.

The Illustrated Police News, December 11, 1869

The Beardless Man

A St Louis woman waked up the other night and putting out her hand touched the smooth face of an unknown man. She jumped out of bed and screamed for help.

Her brother, who slept in the next room, entered, and not finding any matches, seized the intruder by the hair of the head, pummelled him soundly, expressing at the same time in the most vigorous terms, his opinion of a scoundrel who would be guilty of such an act. Then he dragged him into the middle of the room, thumped him, kicked him, and threw him out of the window into the yard below.

The neighbours, aroused by the noise, came in, and a light was procured. Nothing had been taken, and attention was directed to the miserable object who lay groaning in the yard.

It would, says the *St Louis Republican*, be useless to describe that face, with its nose spread all over the middle of it, one eye bulging out and the other closed up, both covered like an indigo bag, an open mouth, and a row of twisted teeth, much less to recognise it: but as the excitement slowly subsided and cool reason began to reign, a thought suddenly struck the wife that made her turn pale with horror. 'Why it can't be – it must be – yes, it is John! He has been to the barber's!'

It was true, he had. He was her husband, and on his way home in the evening, feeling his long and heavy beard oppressive in the heat, he had it shorn. His wife was asleep when he crawled into bed, and he soon fell into a comfortable nap, from which he was rudely awakened to the experience above recorded.

She is now making the best poultices and chicken soup for him she knows how.

*Supplement to the Manchester Courier and
Lancashire General Advertiser*, November 11, 1882

—•—

A Remarkable Story.
Children Confined to a Room for Eighteen Years.

A Leeds contemporary says: A Cleckheaton correspondent who has visited a village less than six miles from York, has been told a strange story, and saw children who had been confined to one room for eighteen years without the knowledge of the villagers.

About twenty-four years ago a woman went to reside in the village with two babies and a girl. The neighbours considered the woman eccentric, and shunned the house. Imagine their surprise when, after the woman's death, they found in a private room two persons – the children of eighteen years before.

They talked rationally, and admitted never having left the room. They had to be taken about the village in a mail cart, and are said to receive the best of everything from the daughters of a millionaire. It is not known who the parents are.

The Yorkshire Gazette, June 10, 1899

Child Buying!

Last Monday a cab proprietor who resides in Belgrave Gate, and whose name begins with a T, happened by some mischance to be in a 'merry mood.'

Not being blessed with any children in his connubial state, as he was passing along Mansfield Street he took a fancy to a child that a woman whom he met was leading, and asked her 'what would she take for the darling?'

The woman replied a sovereign; on which the eager cab-man said 'Done!' and thought he had made a cheap and capital bargain.

The sovereign was readily paid, and the child transferred to the purchaser, who carried off his prize in high spirits to his home, in the blissful anticipation that his 'better half' would give the 'young stranger' welcome greeting.

But alas! his spouse was obdurate, and would not allow the young interloper house room at any price.

He then took the child back to its parents and wanted to get rid of the contract; but they would neither return him his money nor take back the child, telling him he had bought the child and must keep it.

He at last got rid of his 'little responsibility' by giving the parents 5s to take the child back.

The Leicestershire Mercury, April 17, 1847

A Corpse in a House for 20 Years

A curious discovery was made at Birmingham on the 9th inst. An old man, named William Owen, who has been living by himself for the last eight or nine months at Hockley Hill, and been known in the neighbourhood as the 'old miser,' was visited on Wednesday by the relieving officer, as he was in necessitous circumstances.

The officer noticed in one of the rooms a large box, and was informed by Owen, on his being pressed, that it contained the body of his sister, Ellen Perry, who died in Islington Workhouse in 1863.

His sister always had a horror of being buried by the parish, and she was promised by Owen that she should be buried in Birmingham. He had the body enclosed in a zinc and wooden coffin, and brought to Birmingham, where he expected the family to help him defray the expenses of the funeral, but as they did not do so he determined to keep the corpse in the house as long as he lived.

This he had done, and when he moved from one district to another some months ago, the box containing the coffin was taken with the other things.

Owen was always an object of considerable curiosity and suspicion, and for 15 years no one entered his door. He lived in one room, and was never known to have a light in the house.

As the certificate of his sister's death was in Owen's possession, no inquest will be held. The man has been taken to the Workhouse.

The Western Gazette, Yeovil, January 18, 1884

Singular Circumstance Attending the Birth of a Child

A curious incident occurred in a family the other day at Birkenhead, in which a husband actually lost his reason with excessive joy at the announcement that he had become a father.

The man is a joiner, and resides in Brook Street, Birkenhead. It appears that on Monday night last week, he returned home from his work, when he was informed that his 'better-half' had borne him a child.

The circumstance, although by no means unexpected, seemed instantly to produce a most joyous effect upon his mind, for he immediately danced and jumped about the room in a very excited state.

He was then told that his wife required a plaster for her chest, when he hurried to a druggist's shop for the purpose of obtaining it. Whilst in the shop his manner appeared frantic, and after shouting that the police were pursuing him, he rushed out of the premises.

Nothing was heard of the man for two days, although a diligent search was made for him, but on Wednesday night he made his appearance at his own house, and had scarcely entered when the cries of his new-born child were heard, which produced on him the greatest excitement.

Without speaking to any one, he sallied forth into the yard, where he stripped himself of all his apparel, except his shirt and trousers, which he threw into an adjoining yard. He then rushed out of the house, and fled in the direction of Claughton Park, after which he was seen to enter a plantation at Bidston.

Several parties were deputed to endeavour to discover his whereabouts, but although he had been seen rambling about Bidston Hill in his wild and naked state, none of them succeeded in securing him.

On Friday morning, after being worn out with hunger and fatigue, he entered a small cottage at the foot of Bidston, kept by a person named Davies, and requested to be supplied with some milk. An old woman, pitying the forlorn condition of the wretched man, prepared him some bread and milk, which he ate with avidity, after which he again made his way into the plantation.

On the following morning, Davies met the maniac on the top of Bidston, and after a few words of salutation, the latter inquired whether he (Davies) had seen anything of the police. Being replied to in the negative, he asked to be taken to the old woman who had, on the previous day, supplied him with the bread and milk. Davies at once induced him to accompany him to his house, where the old woman again served him with a quantity of food. He was afterwards persuaded to retire to rest, and he slept soundly until 11 o'clock.

At this time the man presented a most wretched aspect, his feet and legs being torn and lacerated by walking amongst the briars in the plantation.

Whilst he was asleep, Davies sent word to his friends, who despatched a cab to convey him home, but he would not consent to leave the house, unless the old woman who had generously supplied him with bread and milk accompanied him.

After reaching the afflicted family, medical assistance was promptly secured, and although he had since suffered much from illness, he is now in a fair way of recovery.

The Kendal Mercury, January 17, 1852

———•———

A London Mystery

Mr Lushington, the Bow Street magistrate, has received a letter from Captain Lewsey, of the Royal Dublin Fusiliers, which tells a very strange story. He states that last Wednesday evening his wife took the 6.30pm train from Newport to London, taking with her her little boy Harold, aged four years.

She arrived at Paddington at 11.40pm, and drove to an hotel. She left the child there, and went out to make some small purchase. She then tried to return to the hotel, but failed to find it.

Though every endeavour has been made to discover the hotel, nothing can be heard of it, and the Scotland Yard authorities, in whose hands the matter has been placed, have been unable to trace the whereabouts of the child.

As a last resource, Capt Lewsey communicated with Mr Lushington, asking that the matter might be mentioned by the Press.

The Leicester Chronicle and Leicestershire Mercury,
September 5, 1896

A Real Romance in Humble Life

Seven years ago, an old Scotchman, named, we believe, Allison, arrived in the township of Underskiddaw, near Keswick, and located himself in Milbeck, at the foot of the majestic Skiddaw.

He obtained work as a labourer from a farmer, and after some time contrived to leave some little money from his earnings in the hands of his employer. One day the old man asked for his cash, saying, 'I have a son in Scotland who could assist me in my work, and I want to bring him here.' The amount was paid and Allison departed, and in a short time returned with his son 'Tom.'

Tom apparently, was an awkward sort of a lad; still he worked with his father in draining and all other kinds of labourers' employment. Some two years ago he worked with a great number of labourers, in deepening Bassenthwaite beck.

Tom, now and then, was apt to show the white feather, and his father would call out, 'Tom, Tom, what ev'r ye aboot? Git on wi' yer work.' The youth's general reply was, 'Mind yer oon.'

The father and son lived together in a cabin quite cosily. Tom was also a frolicsome sort of a fellow; he went in company with the 'lads of the village,' and played off all kinds of nocturnal pranks, sweethearting the girls, drinking his glass, singing his song, and smoking his pipe; nothing came amiss to Tom. He courted, it is said, a young woman for 18 months. Our hero was quite a 'character.'

Tom's career as a young man was not, however, doomed to last for ever, for in the early part of last week 'Tom' unexpectedly gave birth to a fine child, to the astonishment of the whole neighbourhood.

Tom's sex having never once been suspected, his female neighbours would scarcely believe their organs of vision after being called in, even when they found this extraordinary mother suckling the child, from the shortness of the crop of hair and appearing in unmentionables. The old man, we are informed, owns to the paternity of the offspring which has thus brought to light the sex of this rural celebrity. It has been said that since this auspicious event some of those who have occasionally employed Tom are overwhelmed with vexation at the notion of their having paid him from 2s to 3s per day, in place of 1s 6d, a woman's ordinary wage.

The Huddersfield Chronicle, September 13, 1856

◌ FOOD and DRINK ◌

~ *Preface* ~

A recipe for lark pie. Tips on the preparation of eel stew. A comprehensive list of the duties of a footman. Advice for treating someone struck by lightning.

For anyone who required these things in the second half of the nineteenth century, there was one place to turn: Mrs Beeton's *Book of Household Management*, a domestic version of Google, painstakingly compiled over the course of four years by the wife of a prominent publisher.

Within its 2,751 numbered paragraphs, the book dispensed pithy wisdom on the art of dressing a bullock's heart, the practicalities of cleaning plate and whether or not a drowned man should be hung up by his heels. (Not, was the conclusion. Far better to stick him in a bath, then tickle his nose with a feather.)

If you had half a calf's head handy and a partially drained bottle of sherry, Isabella Beeton was there to explain how to fashion them into mock turtle soup. If you needed to brush up on the origin of the onion, she was ready with the answer. And if you'd forgotten how long to boil carrots, a quick flick to the right section would put you right. Ah yes, two and a quarter hours.

To her devoted readership, she represented an ideal of British motherhood, a lighthouse beam to guide them through the rocky waters of etiquette and the expectations of the age.

But though the book is rightly cherished for offering a glimpse of day-to-day home life in the Victorian era, it isn't, of course, anything like the full picture.

To the slum-dwellers of the great cities of Britain, Mrs Beeton's rarefied world was as foreign as the French names of the dishes she recommended for her dinner parties.

Thirty years after the *Book of Household Management* first appeared on bookshelves, Friedrich Engels' *The Condition of The Working Class in England* was finally published in English. Flicking from one to the other is like flipping a flan to find the underside teeming with maggots.

'Among ill-paid workers, even if they have no large families, hunger prevails in spite of full and regular work; and the number of the ill-paid is very large', wrote Engels. 'In these cases all sorts of devices are used; potato parings, vegetable refuse, and rotten vegetables are eaten for want of other food, and everything greedily gathered up which may possibly contain an atom of nourishment.'

Even if they could scrape together the money for some of the more modestly-priced ingredients in Mrs Beeton's recipes, it didn't necessarily follow that the poor had anywhere to cook them. Nor did it mean they knew how to cook. In that, at least, they shared some common ground with the aristocracy. When the Marchioness of Londonderry announced that she knew how to grill a chop, it made the *Illustrated London News*.

There was another sector of society that fell beyond the scope of Mrs Beeton's culinary advice: the unscrupulous. This was a time of wholesale adulteration of food and drink, when milk was diluted with water or thickened with starch, when beer was crafted with strychnine and when red lead lent an appealing hue to cheese.

There must have been quite a surreptitious demand for such sly recipes, but the virtuous Mrs Beeton certainly didn't oblige. Nor, come to think of it, did she explain how to kill and cook a dog for an impromptu victory feast after an election. So the Liberals of West Bromwich, as we shall see, were forced to improvise.

Whisky Corsets – A Singular Fraud

A Canadian correspondent tells a story which reminds one of James Russell Lowell's famous despatch on petroleum smugglers 'with the pectoral proportions of a Juno.'

A novel method of avoiding the Sunday liquor law, he says, was discovered in Montreal about a fortnight ago.

The proprietor of a candy-store was arraigned in the Recorder's Court, charged with 'selling liquor on Sunday out of whisky corsets'. The latter part of the charge astounded the clerk of the court, until the chief of police explained that after some months of effort to detect how liquor was sold on

Sunday in the French quarter of the city, one of his men while in a candy-store saw a man pass the proprietor five cents. The proprietor produced a small rubber tube from under his vest, one end of which the man put to his mouth and sucked.

The officer pounced on the proprietor and a search revealed that the man wore a pair of tin corsets, with doubled space between the inner and outer partitions, holding over a gallon of liquor. To this the tube was attached by a stop-cock.

The customers leaned over the counter, took the tube in their mouth, and sucked until the proprietor thought they had the worth of their money, when the supply was turned off and the tube put back underneath the vest. The police discovered that many a buxom candy-store woman wore similar tank-corsets and did a rushing business with rubber tubes on Sundays.

Warrants are out for several of the ingenious violators of the law.

The Worcestershire Chronicle, February 20, 1892

Extraordinary Poisoning Near Rugby

A most melancholy occurrence has just taken place in a farm house at Ashby St Ledgers, a village on the borders of Northamptonshire.

It appears that Mr William Payne Cowley, a farmer living in that village with his mother (who is a widow) and his brothers, had his sheep dipped, or washed, last week. The object of this dipping or washing is the extermination of vermin, and for this purpose a strong mixture of arsenic and soft soap diluted with water, is used.

On Tuesday morning last, Mr W.P. Cowley sent his brother, Mr Edwin Cowley, to the adjoining town of Daventry, where he purchased 6lb of white arsenic and a barrel of soft soap weighing 30lb.

On the following morning, Mr W.P. Cowley and his mother prepared the sheep dipping mixture, in which some lambs were washed. In this operation Mr Cowley and several of his labourers were employed.

After assisting her son in the preparation of the soap and arsenic, Mrs Cowley proceeded to make a batter pudding for the dinner of her family and the labourers and servants. By some means as yet unaccounted for, it appears that some arsenic must have become mixed with the pudding, for the whole of the persons who partook of it, ten in number, became violently sick just after dinner, and exhibited all the symptoms of being poisoned.

The best medical assistance in the neighbourhood was procured, but one man has already died, and another is not expected to survive; the others are all more or less affected.

The Leeds Mercury, July 16, 1862

Hilarious Burglars

A remarkable siege has just been sustained by a villa at Passy, the owner of which is away in the country.

Three burglarious youths entered the place, and pillaged the house from ground floor to garret. They might have got off with their booty, but the attractions of the larder and the wine cellar were too much for them.

They feasted on the good things which had been left behind by the family, and finished up with Burgundy, champagne, and prime cognac.

Then they lit the gas, danced, became maudlin, and sang songs, the strains of which floated on the night wind and awoke some neighbours, who sent for the police.

Twenty 'agents' of the law surrounded the villa with revolvers cocked. Nevertheless they seemed afraid to move, as the drunken burglars threatened them from the windows, and they were loath to act without the instructions of their Inspector.

That respectable functionary was in bed, and instead of getting up he told the policeman who had called him to keep the house well surrounded until morning.

At an early hour the Inspector rose, and with the aid of his own men, of the milk-distributors, and of the early risers of the locality generally, went into the house and handcuffed the youthful miscreants, who were helplessly intoxicated. They had kept the policemen at bay during the night by exhibiting two rusty swords and a flintlock pistol.

The Dundee Courier and Argus, August 30, 1888

A Drunken Child

On Wednesday morning a child about seven years old was admitted into the East Dispensary, Liverpool, insensible. The boy was the son of an organ grinder, and had gone into a public house for the purpose of making a collection, when several drinks of whiskey were given to him by the customers, and he fell to the ground.

He was attended to by the doctor, remained in the institution a considerable time, and afterwards was taken home by his parents, still suffering from the effects of the spirits he had consumed.

The Citizen, Gloucester,
December 18, 1890

A Priest's Ruse

A clever trick was practised on Wednesday night by Father Nugent, a well-known Catholic priest, in Liverpool. An entertainment was given in the League Hall, Liverpool, in celebration of St Patrick's Day, to about 3,000 persons.

When all had assembled Father Nugent gave orders to close and lock all the doors, and all means of exit were accordingly kept shut until after eleven o'clock, the time at which the public-houses close. Father Nugent is a great promoter of temperance organisations in the town.

The North and South Shields Gazette and Daily Telegraph,
March 20, 1875

'Real Italian' Ice Cream

Some time ago the Lancet published certain startling revelations concerning the loathsome conditions under which ice creams are prepared by Italian vendors in London.

Now, an exhaustive inquiry into the same subject has just been completed by Dr Macfadyen, of the British Institute of Preventive Medicine, and by Mr Colwell, F.I.C. Their report states among other things that microscopical examination revealed the following delectables: Bed bugs, bugs' legs, fleas, straw, human hair, cats' and dogs' hairs, coal dust, woollen and linen fibre, tobacco, scales of epithelium, and muscular tissue.

The Evening Telegraph, Dundee, November 12, 1895

Poisoned Lozenges

Two boys suddenly died at Bradford on Sunday morning. Several others also were taken ill, and it was then ascertained that it was caused by eating peppermint lozenges bought in the market place on the Saturday from a person named Hardaker.

The lozenges had been made by Mr Joseph Neale, of Stone Street, Bradford, wholesale dealer, who had used 40lbs of sugar, and 12lbs of plaster of Paris, as he thought, but which turned out to be 12lbs of arsenic.

Mr Neale had gone to the shop of Mr Hodgson, druggist, of Shipley, near Bradford, and asked for 12lbs of 'daft' or 'alibi', which meant plaster of Paris, used for adulterating lozenges.

Mr Hodgson was ill in bed, and directed the youth to a cask in the cellar, he went and there being two of a similar description, served his customer with arsenic instead of plaster of Paris. By this mode of adulteration, lozenges can be sold at half price.

On Monday afternoon it was ascertained that 12 persons were dead, and that 50 adults and 28 children were ill. A great number of deaths are reported as having taken place in the country towns and villages around Bradford, in some instances three or four persons are dead in one family.

The West Middlesex Advertiser, November 6, 1858

Death in the Pot

A brewer named Hare, residing in the Old Kent Road, was last week fined £200 by the magistrates of Union Hall, for having mixed copperas, opium, and other poisonous ingredients with his beer. By a singular coincidence, the beer in question had been expressly prepared for a beer-shop keeper named Death.

The Leamington Spa Courier, February 16, 1839

Horrible Proceedings at West Bromwich

An instance of most revolting cruelty, with subsequent details equally horrible, has, it is reported, occurred at West Bromwich. It will be remembered that the School Board contest took place on the 27th ult.

The result was made known the following Saturday night, when it transpired that the six nominees of the West Bromwich Liberal Association were elected, with one independent candidate and four out of five Churchmen, thus giving the former a majority of one, which, it may be added, was secured by five votes only. It is stated on reliable authority that a number of men, who denominate themselves Liberals, assembled at a public-house in Spon Lane, West Bromwich, and discussed the means they should adopt to celebrate the 'victory.' Report states that some of the party became intoxicated, and suggested that a dog should be laid upon the table 'for supper.'

Incredible as this may appear the proposal was carried out. A man went to the door of the public-house, and after a few minutes' watching, enticed a dog – a half-bred retriever. This was taken into the house and killed with a *sang froid* air by some of the party.

The next proceeding was to cook the carcase of the unfortunate dog. No difficulties appear to have been considered insurmountable, and it was decided that the animal should be roasted. Accordingly the process of 'drawing' the carcase, as would be done in the case of a hare, was carried out, a portion of the inside being carefully dressed for cooking. Provision for roasting the carcase was obtained, and the cooking was proceeded with, a number of the men watching it with the coolness of cannibals. The dog's liver was fried.

The cooking occupied about an hour, after which the carcase was placed upon a dish and removed to a room prepared to receive the company. The dish was put upon a table before some half-dozen persons, who ate the greater part of the dog's remains, including the liver, all of which appeared to be disposed of with considerable relish. During this time commonplace conversation was indulged in, and the party left the house only when they could remain no longer, and went to their homes. Some of the men have since been too ill to work.

Further Particulars

It appears, from facts which are reported, that the circumstances in connection with the case of dog-eating at West Bromwich are of a more disgusting nature than previously stated.

As already mentioned, the dog was a half-bred retriever. It weighed 36lb. It was removed to the yard at the back of the public-house at which the proceedings are alleged to have taken place; and the means to be adopted for killing the dog having been previously discussed, a thin rope was put round its neck, after which it was suspended from a hook at some distance from the ground.

The little life that remained in the unfortunate animal was then rendered extinct by a blow or blows from a stick. A person expressed a desire to possess the dog's skin. The skin was accordingly removed from the body and given to the man who had asked for it. Next, a man cut up a portion of the remains of the dog, which, it is positively stated, were roasted in front of a fire; and a further statement is to the effect that a man's dinner basin was used to catch what was disgustingly termed the 'gravy.'

The landlady of the house at which the events occurred attempted to extinguish the fire and put an end to the proceedings, but she was prevented from doing so, and the portion of the dog was cooked. The remainder was fried, that which was cooked being eaten. Portions of the dog's limbs were used to create 'fun' by some of the men, who rubbed them over the faces of their companions.

The Illustrated Police News, March 20, 1880

Beer v. Water

At seven o'clock on Friday morning, on the farm of Mr George Melsome, Beacon Hill, near Amesbury, in Wilts, commenced a singular match for £5, lasting all day in broiling hot weather, during which the corn in the district around was being rapidly cut down.

The contest which was under the auspices of the Church of England Temperance Society, was the result of a bet at a public meeting at Salisbury, and was between Mr Terrell, a Wiltshire farmer, who challenged his opponent first, and Mr Abbey, an Oxfordshire farmer and lecturer for the Society.

The issue was who would do the most work in the harvest field, the former drinking beer and the latter water only. Fifteen acres to each 'pitcher' were allowed. The result was that beer won by above an acre. Mr Terrell from the first held a very considerable lead and at four o'clock the ground cleared by him was 15a. 3r. 16p., and by Mr Abbey 14a. 3r.

The farmer who lost has handed over the sum to the Salisbury Infirmary. He pitched 19a. 2r. 26p. in less than twelve hours, against 20a. 2r. 7p. by his opponent.

The effects on his body have been very severe. The ordinary labourer pitches about 12a. in a good day's work. It is proposed to present the winner with a gold medal. So great was the strain on him that at four o'clock he was taken to a wood and 'anointed' with whisky, it is stated.

The Grantham Journal,
September 1, 1883

Celebrating His Death-Feast

Johann Kruger, well-known poacher and wood-stealer, of Neuendorf, near Potsdam, has met his death under circumstances of a very unusual and surprising character.

It appears that the Royal keepers and gendarmerie were on the look out for him by reason of some sylvan dereliction he had recently committed, and that he had therefore taken to the woods, in the so-called Kiefernhaide.

Being hard up for food and liquor, he contrived to steal a large dog and a quart bottle of corn brandy, which stores he conveyed to his hiding place, and there proceeded to make preparation for an *al-fresco* feast and carouse which would have been more appropriate to an Indian scout than to a Prussian poacher.

After he had built up and lighted a huge wood fire he slaughtered the dog, skinned it, and roasted one of its legs, upon which he made a copious meal, washing down the 'friend of man' with deep draughts of fiery spirit.

Having finished this strange repast – the relics of which, clean-picked canine leg-bones and an empty bottle, were subsequently found near the ashes of the extinguished fire – he must have stumbled, all but senseless from intoxication, over the pile of burning wood, and fallen into the flames; for his charred remains were discovered by the Royal foresters next morning literally burnt to cinders with the sole exception of the head, by which he was recognised.

In surfeiting himself with roast dog and raw brandy, Kruger had unconsciously celebrated his own death-feast.

The Shields Daily Gazette and Shipping Telegraph, May 3, 1880

Shocking Death from Eating Putrid Fish

Yesterday afternoon Dr Challice, the deputy coroner, held an inquest at the Woodman Tavern, White Street, Bethnal Green, on the body of Sarah Golding, aged seventy-four years, lately residing at No. 11, Winchester Street, Waterloo Town.

The deceased was a silk winder, and on Wednesday night last she purchased two pieces of fried fish at a shop in Hare Street, Brick Lane, and ate them for supper.

Shortly afterwards she was seized with violent vomiting, when she called a lodger, to whom she admitted that the fish was stinking, but she was so very hungry that she was compelled to eat it.

Mr Thomas Jarvis said the deceased died from congestion of the brain, brought on by violent vomiting and exhaustion through eating unsound fish, which was extensively vended in the neighbourhood among the poor. Verdict, 'Died from eating putrid fish.'

The Era, June 12, 1859

An Extraordinary Glutton

The city of Los Angeles, California, is just now honoured with the presence of an extraordinary glutton.

He is a native of the Grand Duchy of Monaco, and seems to have had an eventful life. At the age of three years he could masticate coarse dried beef, and at nineteen had such a voracious appetite that the Grand Duke, fearing a famine in the small Principality, sent him as one of a purchased quota to Romania, whence he afterwards escaped to the United States.

Immediately on his arrival at Los Angeles he ate 34lb weight of pork, pork fat, train oil, and tallow candles, and subsequently consumed all the cold joints of a good-humoured *restaurateur*, to whom he offered a 25c. stamp to cover the damage.

The citizens of Los Angeles, like all Californians, have a fondness for 'big things,' and the result is that, instead of riding this 'big eater' out of the town on a rail, they have taken hold of him with their accustomed enthusiasm, and now offer to back him for a 'square meal' against the world.

The Manchester Evening News, August 12, 1871

A Curious Incident

A curious accident is reported from Hirson, on the Northern Railway of France. A drunken man named Lefebvre contrived, unobserved, says the London *Daily News*, to mount upon a locomotive, left at the moment unattended at the station in that town, and, turning on the steam, started it down the line at an accelerated pace in the direction of Buire.

Being ignorant of the practical working of the engine the man was powerless to arrest the mischief, and the locomotive, coming into collision with an empty carriage, dashed it to pieces. Finally, it was somehow turned into a siding, where, colliding with violence with the buffers, it was brought to a stand.

Only five minutes later an express train passed down the line. The strangest part of the incident is that the drunken engine-driver is reported to have sustained no serious injury.

The Shields Daily Gazette and Shipping Telegraph,
September 24, 1890

Topics of the Day

A dealer in Connecticut lately sold a bottle of 'the best brandy,' which was handed to Professor Silliman, of Vale College, for analysis. He found it to be concocted on a basis of whisky, with additions of alum, sulphuric acid, an essential oil of some kind, tannic acid, cayenne pepper, burnt sugar, lead, and copper, all of which appear to have been found necessary to produce the peculiar cognac flavour so much admired.

The Western Daily Press, Bristol, January 6, 1872

A Wonderful Stomach

An extraordinary gastronomical feat has been performed at Derby. A man, out of sheer bravado, while in a public house, cut up his fur cap and swallowed the pieces, then he ate up a newspaper, and, as a reward, asked the company for a few coppers.

Five pennies were accordingly thrown to him, and on the suggestion of one of the company, these were sent after the newspaper and the fur cap.

The silly fellow suddenly became ill, and was taken to the infirmary, where he is now paying the penalty for his rash act.

The Shields Daily Gazette and Shipping Telegraph,
May 26, 1882

✒ HEALTH and MEDICINE ✒

~ *Preface* ~

The patient arrived doubled up with pain: breathless, faint and exhausted, clutching her chest, her lips tinged an alarming shade of blue.

Doctors at St George's Hospital in London knew just what to do. They treated her with an ether mixture and a laxative, and finished with a flourish, a new wonder drug that was fresh to the market, having been launched the year before as a cough suppressant.

To scientists it was diacetylmorphine, but the pharmaceutical firm Bayer, seeking a snappier brand name, called it Heroin. You may have heard of it.

The patient, alas, died a few days later, senior physician William Ewart told the annual meeting of the British Medical Association in 1899. Heroin wasn't to blame, but its days as a moreish over-the-counter sedative proved equally short-lived.

Using a powerful narcotic to tackle a cough may seem a tad disproportionate, but this was an era when consumption was rife, and when industrialisation, urbanisation, poverty, overcrowding and poor sanitation conspired to short-change Britons of their allotted three score years and ten in all manner of unpleasant ways.

An age of disease inspired an age of remedies. From

the travelling medicine men of the Wild West to the pages of the local press in Britain, miracle cures were everywhere.

Proof, if it is needed, lies in the British Newspaper Archive. Pick a paper. Any paper. The *Whitstable Times and Herne Bay Herald*, say. On … eeny meeny miny mo … Saturday, February 23, 1889.

On the front, an advertisement for Dr West's Nerve and Brain Treatment promised a catch-all cure for conditions ranging from hysteria to depression to premature old age. 25 shillings bought a box containing six months'-worth of treatment. Expensive, but a small price compared to the 'misery, decay and death' you otherwise risked.

A turn of the page reveals a riot of medicinal adverts, from Clarke's world-famed Blood Mixture for cancerous ulcers and scurvy sores to Holloway's ointment to ease 'bad legs and old wounds' to Electro Galvanic Suspensory Belts, which were just the thing, it seems, for 'night troubles'.

And then there was Dr J. Collis Browne's Chlorodyne, which promised to 'assuage pain of every kind' from toothache to cancer. Dr Gibbon, of the army medical staff in Calcutta, swore by it, according to his frank testimony. 'Nine doses completely cured me of diarrhoea', he crowed, though considering the principal ingredients of Chlorodyne included chloroform, tincture of cannabis and laudanum, it's possible Dr Gibbon wasn't so much cured of diarrhoea as not especially bothered about it any longer.

Prevention, though, was better than cure, and at the

start of Victoria's reign there were a number of medical men who believed one thing in particular needed preventing: pollution. Not the literal kind, but the sort Victorians euphemistically referred to as self-pollution.

'Many physicians of high authority have maintained that two-thirds of the diseases to which the human race is liable have had their origin in certain solitary practices', declared our old friend Eugene Becklard in his *Physiological Mysteries*.

That figure, M. Becklard thought, was fancifully high, but he was pretty certain that consumption, impotence and lunacy were the effects of excessive fondness for one's own company. Females were as keen on the hobby as males, he warned, making use of 'large foreign substances to procure pleasure'.

Ah. Perhaps *that's* why Mrs Beeton recommended boiling carrots for two and a quarter hours.

A Wonderful Recovery

On Saturday at Eastbourne, a tradesman named Thomas Wickens was charged with attempting to commit suicide by driving four long nails into his head.

Dr McQueen produced four long nails which he had with difficulty withdrawn from the head of Wickens. These nails had penetrated three inches, and gone through the brain; but to the surprise of the medical staff at the Memorial Hospital, Wickens had fully recovered.

Wickens said he drove the nails into his head in succession with a hammer, and that he had felt better in his head since the occurrence. He is now sane and able to resume business; and, medically, his recovery is regarded as the most wonderful on record. The magistrate ordered him to be discharged.

The Citizen, Gloucester, August 4, 1890

An Extraordinary Cure

The New York *Sun* gives the story of a cure effected on two violently insane patients in the Hudson County Lunatic Asylum, by the superintendent, Dr George W. King, formerly of Springfield, Massachusetts. His successful experiment was to place the two men together in a cell, each with the instruction to watch the other, who was insane. They sat from morning to night gazing compassionately at each other; in a week they were as quiet as if perfectly sane, and in two months were discharged cured.

The Evening News, Portsmouth, March 15, 1886

A New Way of Pulling Out a Tooth!

The bravest among us often quail at the prospect of a visit to the dentist, and endure a very martyrdom from toothache rather than submit to the extraction of the offending tooth (says the *Evening Standard*).

But when one's courage is screwed to the extracting point, it is evidently to the patient's advantage that the operation should be performed by a skilful hand, rather than by the unpractised one of the sufferer.

A Frenchman residing in the environs of Paris held a contrary opinion, and it is still doubtful whether his error may not cost him his life, owing to the unusual manner in which he played the *role* of dentist.

He had long been suffering from toothache, but obstinately refused to have recourse to a dentist, and at length, finding the pain unendurable, took the following uncommon method of extraction.

To the tooth he attached firmly a long string, to the string a heavy stone, thus armed he proceeded to the topmost storey of the house he occupied, opened the window, and hurled the stone into the air.

The weight of the stone and the length of the string produced so violent a shock, that not only was the tooth pulled out, but with it a portion of the man's jaw, his neck being so painfully twisted that he fainted.

Hours ensued ere consciousness returned. When he ultimately recovered his senses it was found necessary to remove him to a hospital, where he now lies in a most precarious state. Should he quit the hospital a living man, it is hoped he will also be a wiser one.

The Alnwick Mercury, March 2, 1878

Cured by Lightning

A remarkable case of paralysis being cured by lightning is reported from Bad Beyhausen.

A Berlin doctor ordered a patient of his who had been paralysed in both feet for many years to take the baths, not for a cure as that appeared hopeless, but thinking the invalid might possibly derive some slight benefit from the waters.

The patient was ordered to be as much as possible in the open air, and was in the habit of sitting outside the house in a bath-chair.

Recently a violent thunderstorm came on, and everybody in the house forgot the sick man was outside. Suddenly a vivid flash of lightning and a terrific crash of thunder reminded them of the fact, and they were just about to go in search of him when the invalid appeared in their midst, walking without any difficulty. From that moment, he has appeared to be completely cured.

This case, the *Hoyaer Wochenblatt* says, has excited great interest among the medical men; some of whom believe the cure to be effected merely by fear and the intense desire to walk, others think that the electric current may have assisted the paralysed limbs to move.

The Huddersfield Daily Chronicle, September 7, 1891

Strange Adventure

A correspondent writes to a contemporary: 'An Oxfordshire woman met with an experience a few days back which should act as a warning to intending visitors to lunatic asylums.

'The person in question journeyed to Littlemore, a village four miles distant from Oxford where there is an asylum, with the intention of visiting a female patient. The porter, having admitted her, is said to have duly passed her on to one of the matrons with the words "to visit a female patient;" but the nurse appears to have caught only the last words of the sentence, and a mistake resulted which cost the visitor a good deal of unpleasantness, to say the least of it.

'The stranger was taken to the top of the building, under the belief that she was going to see her friend, and then she was suddenly shut into an empty room. Shortly afterwards a nurse entered, and, to the consternation of the visitor, at once proceeded to undress her. Protestations and remonstrances were alike unavailing, and firmly, though not unkindly, the poor woman was stripped and placed in a bath, after which she was forcibly put to bed.

'By this time the mistaken lunatic was of course in a frantic state of alarm, which only favoured the belief that she was really a mad woman. Where the gruesome farce might have ended it is not pleasant to contemplate; but by a lucky accident the mistake was discovered later in the day, and the unfortunate woman was set at liberty with profuse apologies.

'It is satisfactory to hear, under the circumstances, that no complaint has been made as to undue severity on the part of the nurses.'

The Western Daily Press, Bristol, November 15, 1884

Singular Accident and Extraordinary Cure

On Saturday afternoon an accident, which was nearly proving fatal, happened to a man named Adam Drewe, employed at the Ironworks, Seend, near Melksham.

It appears that the large iron tube, about thirty feet in circumference, through which hot air is blown from the engine, sometimes gets obstructed by ashes, and then a man has to creep into it for the purpose of removing them. This was the case on Saturday, and Drewe, who is a powerfully-built man, got into the tube for the above purpose.

Not making his re-appearance, a man was sent into the tube to search for him, and found him jammed in a narrow part of the tube, in an insensible state. After some difficulty he was pulled out, still insensible, with several scars and burns on his body.

Now comes the most extraordinary part of the story – the Staffordshire mode of bringing him to life, and it was as follows: A hole was dug in the ground large enough to receive Drewe's head, and into this hole his head was put, face downwards, and carefully covered up in the 'mother earth,' with the exception of a small hole left when breathing time came.

Wonderful to relate, there were soon signs of returning life, and Drewe so far recovered as to 'unearth' himself. Brandy was administered to him, and he was soon himself again.

The Grantham Journal, October 25, 1873

Cocaine in Hay Fever

The therapeutical uses of cocaine are so numerous that the value of this wonderful remedy seems only beginning to be appreciated. Almost daily we hear of some disease or combination of symptoms in which it has been tried for the first time and has answered beyond expectation.

It appears strange that so intractable a complaint as hay fever should be amenable to its influence, and yet such is the case. The account given by Mr Watson, of the Westminster Hospital of his sufferings and subsequent cure by tabloids of cocaine, is too circumstantial to admit of doubt, even had we not received confirmatory evidence from many sources.

It has been objected on theoretical grounds that cocaine must of necessity be inoperative, or at all events of comparatively little use, in those cases in which symptoms of an asthmatic type prevail.

Curiously enough, however, it has been shown that cocaine, when applied to the mucous membrane of the nostrils, has the power of allaying even this spasm. The observation, too, is not new; for many months ago Dr Bosworth, professor of laryngology at Bellevue Hospital Medical College, published a detailed account of a case of spasmodic asthma completely cured by cocaine. He pointed out at the time that many inveterate cases of asthma are dependent on, or at all events associated with, nasal disorders, the relief of which is promptly followed by an abatement of all the distressing symptoms. If this principle of associated treatment should be carried on in its integrity, it will be difficult to assign the limits of its sphere of action.

The Manchester Evening News, July 18, 1885

Extraordinary Cure of Blindness

A correspondent of the *Sheffield Telegraph* writes: A most extraordinary cure of blindness has recently taken place to a gardener named Geo. Parker, aged 82, who resides at Rose Cottage, Brimington, near Chesterfield. He has been troubled with cataracts and nearly totally blind.

The old man in May last dreamed that he had been applying petroleum to his eyes and had recovered his sight. His sons and the doctor advised him not to try the experiment, fearing it would injure the eyes. He, however, last August commenced to rub petroleum over the right eye, and persevered with his treatment till in the course of a week or 10 days the right eye was restored to its former state.

He then commenced the same operation on the left eye, which had been blind for six years, and in 14 days from his first applying it was able to see a little with that one, but it was feared that the cataract being on the left eye so long it has affected the inner portion of the sight. The right eye still remains perfectly clear, and it has been pronounced by four doctors to be one of the most extraordinary cures on record.

The Manchester Courier and Lancashire General Advertiser,
October 21, 1881

A Home-Coming and Thanksgiving

An aged couple in Medway, Mass., had a merry thanksgiving. At the outbreak of the war their only son ran away to sea, and served under Farragut at New Orleans and with Cushing in the Albemarle exploit.

Here all trace of the sailor was lost, and it was supposed that he was drowned in the river when the torpedo exploded. His sister died a few years ago, and his parents have been living in retirement and poverty.

Late one night a man with a scar on his face knocked at the door and requested a lodging. He was admitted by the old lady, who asked her aged husband to entertain the stranger while she was making a cup of tea for him. The stranger kept his hat on, and the old lady noticed that his eyes followed her every movement.

To the old man he represented that he had formerly lived in the neighbourhood. When asked his name he gave an evasive answer, but asked if James Merrisk lived there yet. 'I am James Merrisk,' answered the old man.

The old lady had been watching the stranger closely. Before he could utter another word she stepped quickly to his side, lifted the hat from his head, gazed a moment to his face, and sank into the arms outstretched to receive her, loudly screaming 'Jim! Our Jim!'

'Yes, your Jim; come home for thanksgiving,' exclaimed the stranger, as he kissed the aged face with joy and turned to his father, whose frame was trembling with gratitude.

After a while he related the eventful history of his wanderings. He had been severely wounded by the explosion of the torpedo, as the scar on his face testified. He was pulled from the river by one of the boats which came to the relief of the crew of the Albemarle.

He lost his senses by the concussion and wound, but after the latter healed he was permitted to go at large as harmless, knowing nothing of himself, not even his name. Finally he fell into the employ of a former surgeon of the rebel army, and with him went to a plantation outside of Raleigh, N.C.

One day, however, the surgeon examined his wound and determined to try an experiment. He opened the wound in the head, and found the skull fractured and pressing in the brain. With the aid of another surgeon the skull was lifted or trepanned, and the wound again closed gradually. Merrisk's condition improved, but it was fully a year before his memory returned.

The Grantham Journal, January 3, 1880

A Wonderful Recovery after 65 Years a Deaf Mute.

Dr Livingstone, a resident of the little village of Bennetsville, Chenango County, N.Y., has regained the power of speech and hearing after having been a deaf mute for nearly 65 years.

His wonderful recovery has excited much comment, and is regarded by many as a miracle. The old man is very well known in his own as well as adjoining counties. One night about two weeks ago he awoke in the night with a severe pain in his head, as if he had been struck with a club.

He called out to his wife, who was sleeping beside him. At the sound of his voice she awoke, astonished to hear him pronounce her name. She had never before heard him speak. As soon as she recovered from her surprise she asked him what was the matter. Her words were the first he had heard since he was an infant, and the revelation of his changed condition astounded him.

The pain in the meantime felt less acute, and he and his wife talked until morning of his wonderful recovery. The news spread quickly, and all the next day the doctor was overwhelmed with congratulations.

Conversation at first caused him great annoyance, but he has gradually become accustomed to it. His vocabulary, which at first was limited, has increased, and he has no difficulty in expressing himself. When Dr Livingstone was three years old a severe attack of scarlet fever left him entirely deaf. The few childish words he knew gradually were forgotten, and by the time he was six years old he became a mute.

Despite his past affliction the old man is intelligent and well-read. He is at a loss to account for his strange good fortune, and the physicians in the neighbourhood can shed no light on the mystery.

Dr Livingstone is anxious to have his case investigated by the medical fraternity in hope that some explanation as to his recovery can be given. The pain which he felt in his head gradually passed down his spine into his legs and then left him entirely. Though 71 years old he is in excellent health.

The Sunderland Daily Echo and Shipping Gazette,
July 14, 1893

———

A New Disease

Attention has lately been drawn in one of our medical contemporaries to a disease met with in Siberia, known to the Russians by the name of 'Miryachit.'

The person affected seems compelled to imitate anything he hears or sees, and an interesting account is given of a steward, who was reduced to a perfect state of misery by his inability to avoid imitating everything he heard and saw.

One day the captain of the steamer, running up to him, suddenly clapping his hands at the same time, accidentally slipped and fell hard on the deck. Without having been touched, the steward instantly clapped his hands and shouted; then, in helpless imitation, he, too fell as hard and almost precisely in the same manner and position as the captain.

This disease has been met with in Java, where it is known as 'Lata.' In the case of a female servant who had the same irresistible tendency to imitate, one day at dessert her mistress, wishing to exhibit this peculiarity, and catching the woman's eye, seizing a large French plum, made pretence to swallow it whole.

The woman rushed at the dish and put a plum in her mouth, and, after severe choking and semi-asphyxia, succeeded in swallowing it, but her mistress never tried the experiment again.

The Western Daily Press, Bristol, June 25, 1884

Curious Cure For Insanity

Mrs Teresa Nally, wife of John Nally, a New York truckman, shot herself recently while insane. She had made many previous attempts to destroy herself.

Mrs Nally found the rifle, loaded it, placed the muzzle under her chin, and pressed the trigger with her toe. The bullet bored through her chin and tongue, and perforating the roof of her mouth, lodged in the brain.

The coroner, who took her ante-mortem statement, found that she had recovered her senses. She told him clearly and in an intelligent manner that she had been in ill-health for a long time, and had undergone a serious operation.

Commitment papers have been made out, and she is to be taken to the Long Island State Hospital, at King's Park. 'But I'm not crazy now,' she said, 'the bullet has cured me. I may die, but I won't die crazy.'

The Worcestershire Chronicle, January 27, 1900

A Dumb Man Cured by Excitement

A curious 'cure' is exciting much interest in medical circles, as well as among the general public, in Germany. A twelvemonth ago a Bavarian cattle-dealer was kicked by a horse, with the result that he became quite dumb.

A day or two ago he was riding a horse to its fate in the knacker's yard, when the animal suddenly began to plunge and kick. The man, taken by surprise, lost his head in wild excitement, and after a few moments began to talk, and completely regained language, to the boundless astonishment of his friends.

The Evening Telegraph, Dundee, August 9, 1895

An Octogenarian and his Drugs

Mr Coates, of Boston, Massachusetts, the millionaire, who intends bequeathing his collection of drugs to the University of Boston, gathered them together in rather a curious way.

He has reached the age of 83 years without ever having taken any medicine. It must not be thought, however, that he never called in medical men; on the contrary, he seems to have had recourse to his doctor whenever he had the slightest ailment. He had all the prescriptions religiously executed at the chemist's.

Only, he never swallowed the drugs, but carefully put them away in his cupboard, and today he finds himself the possessor of a most original collection – 1,900 bottles of sundry medicines, 1,370 boxes of various powders, and 870 boxes of pills.

The Evening Telegraph, Dundee, September 8, 1894

Curious Cure for Headache

A noted physician has, it is said, met with great success in his treatment of persistent cases of 'nervous' headaches, and he has finally disclosed the secret. In each case, he says, after the patient had laid bare a long tale of woe – of sleepless nights and miserable days – he prescribed, briefly, a simple hair cut.

It is not necessary that the hair should be cropped-off short, after the fashion of convicts. The curative property of the treatment is based on the fact that the tube which is contained in each single hair is severed in the process, and the brain 'bleeds,' as the barbers say, thereby opening a safety valve for the congested cranium.

The Lincolnshire Chronicle, June 2, 1896

Remarkable Determination of a Boy.
Cutting Off His Own Finger

A Galashiels correspondent telegraphs: An extraordinary occurrence took place near here on Sunday. A boy named Brockie, the son of a shepherd at Buckholm, was out with the sheep when he was bitten on the finger by an adder.

He became alarmed lest the bite should prove fatal, and resolved to cut the finger off close to the palm. This he attempted to do with his pocket-knife, but as it would not cut through the bone he cut it away at the first joint. He then went to the nearest farmhouse, whence he was driven to Galashiels. Here a doctor amputated the remainder of the finger. The lad refused to take chloroform, and, although weak is doing well.

The Evening Telegraph and Star, Sheffield,
August 25, 1891

Paris 'Pigeon' Cure.
An Extraordinary Superstition

If the following facts, writes a Paris correspondent, were not vouched for by a highly distinguished physician, Dr G. Legue, it would be permissible to regard them as an invention suggested by sundry of the marvellous 'cures' in vogue in the Middle Ages.

Dr Legue was put on the track of his curious discovery by one of his patients, who informed him in the most casual manner, and as if there were nothing extraordinary about the statement, that she had tried the 'pigeon cure' for meningitis, and for the first time with limited success. Dr Legue had to confess his entire ignorance of the cure in question, and to ask for an explanation of its nature.

It was then revealed to him that in this sceptical age, and in Paris, of all places in the world, there are people who believe in the efficaciousness, as a remedy for certain maladies, of the blood of a freshly killed pigeon.

The head of the patient to be treated is shaved, and then the breast of the pigeon is ripped open by the 'operator,' and the warm and bleeding carcase immediately applied to the bared skull.

The believers in this cruel and senseless cure imagine that all fever is drawn out of the body by the hot life blood and the quivering flesh of the pigeon. The extraordinary thing is that faith in the cure is widespread, and recourse to it frequent.

Dr Legue, who had thoroughly investigated the matter, has been able to obtain the address of the shop in the Central Markets at which nothing else is sold but live pigeons destined to this strange purpose. The business done is so brisk that the late proprietor, Mme. Michel, has been able to retire, after making a small fortune.

Her successor declares that the pigeon cure is considered a sovereign remedy for influenza, since the appearance of which she has been unable to meet the demand that has arisen for birds. They are also used, it seems, in cases of typhoid fever, but in this instance two pigeons are necessary, and they are applied to the feet of the patient.

The Evening Post, Dundee, February 15, 1900

✎ COINCIDENCE and LUCK ✎

∼ *Preface* ∼

They buried the Truby boys in one grave. Three brothers, side by side in the Pennsylvanian dirt.

They'd died within twelve hours of each other; three lives snuffed out in three separate accidents that brought three separate messengers to their bewildered mother's door.

Railwayman John was the first to go, breaking his neck on a summer's night in 1885 when he tripped while running to change the points on the track. Before word of his death reached home, his brother Jason stumbled into a quarry pit filled with rainwater, striking his head as he fell. The news arrived in their village just as the body of their older brother Wyman was being carried out from the mill where he worked. He'd suffocated in a grain silo.

Just when you think this desolate story couldn't get much worse, the newspaper report turns to the widowed Mrs Truby, concluding with one of the most cheerless closing sentences of the century: 'The succession of cruel blows so overwhelmed her that she is not expected to live.'

Coincidence was a recurring theme in the work of many of the nineteenth century's greatest authors, and a regular motif in newspapers of the era too. At a time when science was hacking away at the old certainties, the Victorians liked to savour life's surprises.

And some of them liked it to an irksome extent. An article in the *New Monthly Magazine* in 1852 tore into the types who saw parallels wherever they looked. 'The life of the coincidentalist is a perpetual succession of wonders, though nothing after all is new to him. If you mention to him some casual circumstances, too trivial for remembrance beyond the moment of its occurrence, he receives it like an old acquaintance. He finds a subject for comparison in everything and nothing happens that is not extraordinary, surprising or remarkable.'

There must have been a fair few of them working in journalism. A search for the phrase 'singular coincidence' in the British Newspaper Archive throws up more than 10,000 articles.

Extraordinary Occurrence

An extraordinary coincidence is reported as having occurred in Dublin Bay. The other morning two Ringsend fishermen, named James Hodgens and George Roden, were fishing in a trawler about six miles east of Howth when, on drawing in the net, they were horrified to find that it contained the body of a man.

On the remains being pulled into the trawler the features were examined and one of the men, Roden, discovered the body to be that of his own brother, who was also a fisherman, and who was drowned in the bay on the 14th December, 1890.

The Star, Guernsey, December 8, 1891

Father and Son Killed by Mare and Foal

About twelve months ago a groom in the employ of a gentleman at Dyserth, near Rhyl, was kicked to death by a mare belonging to his employer, who at once, of course, got rid of the brute.

The employer took the deceased's son into his service in a similar capacity, and now the news has come to hand that the son has himself been kicked to death by the foal of the mare that kicked his father to death.

The Citizen, Gloucester, March 29, 1895

Death Under Remarkable Circumstances

A man named Robert Hill met with a shocking death under peculiar circumstances at Rochester on Wednesday night. He was a night man under the Corporation and a year ago was principal witness as to the death of a fellow-workman, who drank carbolic acid in mistake for cold tea while at work, and died in consequence.

Notwithstanding this warning, Hill himself on Thursday

morning swallowed a dose of the acid in mistake for whiskey, and died in great agony. He was a married man and about 35 years old.

The York Herald, September 28, 1889

The Extraordinary Fog.
Three Men Killed Near Glasgow

Information reached Glasgow last evening that during the fog yesterday morning while Patrick Murtha, 26, and James Leary, 37, were laying fog signals on the Helensburgh branch of the North British Railway they were overtaken by a train from Helensburgh and cut to pieces.

Shortly afterwards their remains were found by Patrick Reilly, surfaceman, who returned to Maryhill to give information of the occurrence. He afterwards walked back along the line, and on stepping out of the way of a mineral train was killed by a passenger train.

The Aberdeen Journal, January 14, 1888

An Incredible Piece of Luck

It would be difficult to find in the pages of fiction anything to equal the following prosaic fact, which has just happened in Scotland.

A Captain Heathcote rents a moor from year to year. Last year while out shooting he lost a diamond ring. This year he was reminded of it by the anniversary of his loss, and sitting by the fire and taking up a piece of peat to put on, he had scarcely uttered the words, 'It is a year today since I lost my diamond ring,' than his companion was surprised to hear the words quickly followed by 'And here it is.'

The peat had been cut from the very moor where the loss had occurred, and hence its recovery. No other account of extraordinary recovery of diamonds could equal that, unless, perhaps, that of a lady who dropped a diamond into a pond and found it some months after on the leaf of a water-lily which had borne it upwards in its growth.

The Evening Telegraph, Dundee,
September 8, 1894

Singular Coincidence

A woman named Ellen Hoyle walked into the canal at Shipley during fog, on Wednesday. She had given evidence the same day at an inquest on Frank Seed, labourer, who was drowned under similar circumstances.

The Shields Daily Gazette and Shipping Telegraph,
February 27, 1891

Vicar and Church Struck by Lightning

The Rev. F.W. Keene, vicar of Misson, near Bawtry, was struck by lightning eleven weeks ago, and so seriously injured that it was feared he would not recover.

However, the rev. gentleman sufficiently improved to enable him to leave home for a short time for the re-establishment of his health. This was happily effected to a great extent, and it was hoped that he would have been able to resume his duties on Sunday, while his home-coming was to have been celebrated by bell-ringing and other rejoicings.

Unfortunately lightning again played an important and an unpleasant part in the proceedings, for, on the previous day, the church was struck during a storm and set on fire, and the greater portion of it destroyed. Instead of Mr Keene being welcomed by a merry peal from his church bells, he found the edifice an utter wreck.

The Citizen, Gloucester, September 26, 1893

A Singular Coincidence

To the editor of the *Cheshire Observer*.

Sir,

The following coincidence appears to me to be worth recording. Last Sunday morning Samuel Whitehead, a Willaston labourer, whose wife is an inmate of the Upton Asylum, was about to start to Upton for the purpose of seeing her, when he received a letter addressed 'S. Whitehead, Willaston,' informing him that his wife had completely recovered, and that her clothing must be sent at once to the relieving officer. The poor fellow was overjoyed, and on Monday morning sent off her clothing as desired to the relieving officer at Bebington. There, however, he learned to his bitter disappointment that it was the wife of another S. Whitehead, of Willaston, near Crewe, who was referred to, and that his own wife was no better.

Your, &c,
Sympathizee.

The Cheshire Observer, May 30, 1885

Coincidence Extraordinary

A singular coincidence of events has recently occurred at Ely, where a Mr Thomas Ellis finding his last hour was approaching sent a message to that effect to his friend Mr John Kester, who was also in declining health, and the reply was 'Tell my old friend I shall not be long after him.'

Within one hour both were dead. They were born on the same day and hour, and died on the same day and hour, aged seventy-five.

The Grantham Journal, January 30, 1869

Romance of a Warship

A telegram from Montreal describes a romantic incident of the Tourmaline's stay. Among the visitors to the ship was a pretty young girl who met a gallant blue jacket by the name of Charles Moore.

In comparing experiences while he was shewing her about the ship, they made the interesting discovery that they were brother and sister. They are orphans, and were placed in an asylum in London in their early childhood.

Eleven years ago she was sent to Canada by an immigration society, and the boy was placed on a training ship. They lost all knowledge of each other until the discovery made by their meeting.

An unfortunate termination to the romance was caused by Moore's anxiety to see more of his sister. He begged for leave, but was refused, and when he jumped over-board to swim ashore was brought back and placed in irons.

The Whitstable Times and Herne Bay Herald,
October 3, 1891

Calamity at Washington.
400 Killed and Injured.

A shocking catastrophe, which constituted also a very remarkable coincidence, occurred at Washington yesterday morning. While the funeral of the late Edwin Booth was taking place in New York, Ford's Theatre, in which, 28 years ago, the great actor's brother, John Wilkes Booth, shot President Lincoln, collapsed, burying in its ruins all who were at the time within its precincts.

The tragedy enacted in the theatre more than a quarter of a century ago was a memory which had over-shadowed the life of the popular actor since, and it is nothing short of a startling coincidence that at the very moment his remains were being borne from a New York church, amid crowds of sorrowing friends and admirers, the building which had been associated with so sombre a reminiscence in his career should have disappeared with serious attendant consequences.

The Lincolnshire Echo, June 10, 1893

A Fisherman's Luck

On Friday afternoon, shortly after four o'clock, a butcher named Burrows, in the employ of Mr William Harris, of West Smithfield, was fishing in the Grand Surrey Canal when he came upon a very remarkable discovery.

Upon pulling his fishing line out of the water, he found hanging on to the hook a lady's fancy leather hand-bag, which upon being opened was found to contain 39 gold wedding and keeper rings, and £23 in gold and silver. The bag was very old, and judging from its rotten condition, had evidently been under water some considerable time.

The Sunderland Daily Echo and Shipping Gazette,
July 18, 1892

Where the Gold Spoon Went To

A curious story is told by Lady Middleton of how one of Queen Victoria's smallest gold spoons was lost and found. A lady attended a State Ball in a dress the skirt of which was arranged in perpendicular pleats in front, stitched across at intervals, and, unknown to her, a gold teaspoon got lodged at supper in one of these receptacles.

Of course, there was one missing after the ball, and it caused great perturbation to the official in charge of the gold plate. The next spring the lady who had been the innocent cause of the loss went to a Drawing Room in the identical dress she had worn at the State Ball, and as she bent low before Her Majesty the pleats of her skirt expanded, and the gold spoon fell at the Queen's feet!

The Evening Telegraph, Dundee, August 12, 1897

Treasure Trove

Paris, Thursday: An old and dilapidated safe was bought at a public auction here yesterday for a few francs. On opening it the purchaser discovered a secret drawer, in which a sum of 3,000 francs in bank notes was concealed. By law the money becomes the property of the purchaser, and cannot be claimed by the vendor of the safe.

The Evening Telegraph, Dundee, August 25, 1898

An Awkward Change of Name

There are in France two brothers with the surname of Assassin, who recently obtained the necessary permission from the high functionary called the Keeper of the Seals to change their name to one less offensive. After mature reflection, they decided to change their name to Berge.

Now that it is too late to alter it, they have discovered, to their intense annoyance, that their new name happens, by a singular coincidence, to be that of the chief assistant to M. Deibler, the public executioner, who will, in all probability, succeed to M. Deibler's gruesome business.

The Devon and Exeter Daily Gazette, October 18, 1895

Extraordinary Coincidences

One of the most singular coincidences ever recorded has just taken place at a village named Martin's Valley, in Pennsylvania, where three brothers of the name of Truby, all following different trades, met with accidental deaths between 11 o'clock on the night of Friday, August 14, and 11 o'clock on the following morning.

The first killed was John, aged 34, who was a signalman on the railway. He was running to alter a switch, when he fell over something on the line, and broke his neck.

Jason Truby, aged 36, worked in a slate quarry four miles from the village. The recent rains had filled several deep cavities in the quarry with water. Early on Saturday morning Jason went to work. A narrow hemlock board had been laid across one of the pits full of water, and he was walking over it when it tipped with him and threw him into the water. His head came in contact with the edge of the stones, stunning him, and he was drowned before aid could reach him.

Wyman Truby, 38 years old, was a miller. He worked near his mother's house. About half-past ten o'clock on Saturday morning he was at work in the mill, when the flooring of a grain bin in the room above him gave way, and he was buried beneath hundreds of bushels of wheat. A boy who was in the mill ran out and gave the alarm, and several men hurried in and made efforts to extricate Truby; but the work could not be done in time. When he was taken out he had been dead some time.

The brothers died in ignorance of each other's death, and the messengers sent to inform their mother, a widow, met at her house. The succession of cruel blows so overwhelmed her that she is not expected to live.

The Edinburgh Evening News,
September 2, 1885

৩ SPORT, HOBBIES ৩
and PASTIMES

~ Preface ~

If things had turned out a little differently, the list of sports that Britain gave to the world might have needed a single, significant revision. Scrub out football; replace it with egg hat.

The beautiful game was an ugly duckling at the start of the nineteenth century. 'It seems to have fallen into disrepute and is but little practised', wrote Joseph Strutt in *The Sports and Pastimes of the People of England* in 1801. Four decades on, the *Boy's Treasury of Sports, Pastimes and Recreations* could refer to football as a once-popular old English game.

But egg hat, said the *Boy's Treasury* – now there was a sport. A game of skill, speed and agility that involved a ball, some hats and a taste for casual violence.

The rules were pleasingly simple. You put down your hats and a player threw a ball into one. There was some general darting about. A winner was declared, then everyone gathered round in a mood of post-match bonhomie and pelted the loser with balls at close range.

In his 1869 book *The Business of Pleasure*, the author Edmund Hodgson Yates reflected fondly on the 'stinging cuts' inflicted by the game in his childhood, and it's not hard to see why it appealed to the early Victorians, as it combined athleticism, the open air, a will to win and a blithe disregard for the lot of the loser.

As it turned out, egg hat went the way of earlier British pastimes like bear-baiting and chucking sticks at cockerels. Yet for all the games that didn't last the course, the 1800s were a staggeringly productive era.

Inspired by the doctrine of muscular Christianity, which held that manliness was next to Godliness, the Victorians embraced sport, laying the foundations for the professional set-ups we know today. They standardised games that once varied like accents across the country. They formalised rules. They set up leagues, built stadiums and made professionals and celebrities of players.

They even revived the Roman tradition of matchday aggro. Punch-ups and pitch invasions became increasingly common at the football. There were brawls at the rugby and the racing too. A wrestling match in Plymouth in 1879 ended with hundreds of fans smashing the venue's seats. Even the genteel world of cricket wasn't entirely immune. A match between Surrey and Nottinghamshire at the Oval in 1887 was marred by spectators surging on to the field, where they fought a battle plucked from the imagination of Enid Blyton. Or as *The Graphic* put it: 'engaged in a Homeric strife among themselves with ginger-beer bottles and pieces of turf.'

Singular Match at Cricket.
Arms Versus Legs

A match, which, for its novel character, attracted an immense number of spectators, was played last week in the cricket-ground of the Railway Tavern, at Reading.

The players on one side consisted of eleven with only one arm each, while, on the other side, each had but one leg – saving a wooden one. One of the umpires had lost both his arms, and the other had 'not a leg to stand upon.' A referee was also selected who had neither arms nor legs.

At the commencement of the play the 'odds' were in favour of the one-arms; notwithstanding the single-legs had many backers. During the first innings, in consequence of the soft nature of the ground from the late rains, no less than three legs were broken; but these were soon 'set' without the aid of a medical man, a neighbouring carpenter skilfully performing the 'operation.'

At the termination of the game the score stood thus: The single-legs, first innings, 25; second innings, 46; total, 71. The one-arms, first innings, 50; second innings, 60; total, 110. The players dined between the innings at the Railway Tavern.

The Leicester Chronicle, July 19, 1845

A Football as a Detective

Recently, at a match in the North of England, a curious incident happened. A player gave the ball so strong a kick that it went through the net of the opponents' goal, and struck a spectator in the face. The injured man fell down, and was carried to the pavilion.

As he was recovering very slowly the doctor who attended him searched his pockets to find out his name and to enable him to inform the injured man's friends.

Instead of the doctor finding out any name and address, however, he found over a dozen gold watches, one of which belonged to his daughter. Naturally his suspicions were aroused, and he communicated with the police.

When the man recovered he was marched off to the police-station, where it was discovered he was a well-known thief, who had successfully baffled the police for some time. But for the football's blow he wouldn't have been discovered.

The Leeds Times, January 7, 1899

A Strange Adventure

A curious canoe adventure is reported from Frankfurt. Some members of the boat club in that city resolved to row to Mayence by night. They started at 12 o'clock, and pulled away vigorously all night, enjoying the pull exceedingly.

At sunrise it was discovered to their great chagrin that the anchor had not been weighed, and that they had remained at the same spot where they had taken leave of their friends, by whom they are now known as 'the explorers.'

The Evening News, Portsmouth, November 4, 1882

Extraordinary Termination to a Foot Race

Two athletes, named Radcliffe and McDowell, ran a race at Belfast on Saturday. The course was strange to them and they did not know that Prince's Dock intervened between the starting-point and winning-post.

Accordingly, when in the full heat of the race, they came to the dock, and, unable to stop, fell over into the water. They were rescued by the harbour police in an exhausted state.

Supplement to the Northampton Mercury, February 13, 1886

Extraordinary Scene at a Football Match

At a football match, played at Worksop on Saturday, between Beighton and Worksop, the ball was kicked over the hedge into the garden adjoining the football field, and was promptly seized by the wife of the owner of the garden and locked up in an outhouse.

The players, being without a ball, were unable to proceed with the game – another ball having been seized by the same party just before the match commenced and taken to the police station.

One of the players and a spectator went to the proprietor of the garden and his wife and asked for the ball, which was refused, whereupon the two decided to help themselves and accordingly made for the door of the outhouse.

The proprietor of the garden picked up his garden fork and ran at one of them with it, but the latter seeing his danger caught the gardener by the neck, twisted him round, and took the fork from him.

Meanwhile the gardener's wife had not been idle. She armed herself with the swill bucket and battered it about the head of the player who had ventured to seek the ball. This roused the ire of the spectators, who rushed in scores over the hedge into the garden, but seeing the player coming from the garden with the ball under his arm, they retired, otherwise the proprietors of the garden might have fared badly.

As it was, the spectators contented themselves by hooting at the two in the garden till the match terminated.

The Derby Daily Telegraph, April 18, 1887

Extraordinary Cricket Craze.
The Game to be Prohibited

A cricket mania has broken out in the sunny isles of the Pacific. 'Cricket,' writes a colonial newspaper correspondent from Samoa, 'which was introduced here a few years ago by some of the more energetic British residents, has now become a nuisance, owing to the manner in which it is played by the natives.

'It is no uncommon thing to see a game being played in which the players number from 80 to 150 a side, and which lasts for ten days or a fortnight.

'The natives have become so crazy over cricket that they neglect their food crops during the whole of the season, and the consequence is that during a great part of the year they are in a state of poverty.'

King Malietoa is now seriously considering the absolute prohibition of our national game within his dominions.

The Citizen, Gloucester, June 16, 1890

Cricket Match on the Ice

Teams representing the respective cricket clubs of Saddington and Kibworth, two villages just outside Market Harborough, met in an extremely novel encounter on Saddington Reservoir, and an amusing cricket match on ice ended in a draw.

The match was played on skates, and the ice being in splendid condition the 'leather hunting' was very considerable and many 'boundaries' were scored.

Saddington went in first, and although their first man was dismissed by the first ball delivered the team was not disposed of till 205 (28 extras) had been compiled. Smith, a Kibworth bowler, took four wickets in one over. The first two Kibworth men scored 95 without being separated, but at this point of the game the match was declared drawn, owing to the failing light.

The Illustrated Police News, January 14, 1893

Golfer Creates a Panic

One of the most remarkable golf matches on record took place in the streets of Pittsburgh on Saturday, says a New York correspondent.

Several members of the Alleghany Club wagered four thousand dollars that a golf ball could be driven over four miles and a half of the city streets in 150 strokes.

William Patten, a well-known player, was selected to make the test. The course was from the Alleghany Club to the Pittsburgh clubhouse. The first mile was the hardest to cover, fifty strokes being required.

Patten finally sent a ball through the bedroom window of a prominent citizen, and caused a great disturbance. Another went through the window of a tramway car, and created a panic among the passengers.

The entire four miles and a half were finally covered in 119 strokes. Patten finished by landing a ball through the window of the Pittsburgh clubhouse, and still had 31 strokes to spare. Three balls were lost, three clubs were broken, and about £100 worth of damage was done.

The Falkirk Herald and Midland Counties Journal,
July 28, 1900

Singular Prize Fight

A prize fight between a man with one arm and another with one eye took place near Cossington, a secluded part of Leicestershire, on Sunday evening week, in the presence of a large number of spectators, who arrived in sections.

The fight lasted one hour and forty-five minutes, and was of a most determined nature. The one-eyed man had his eye so

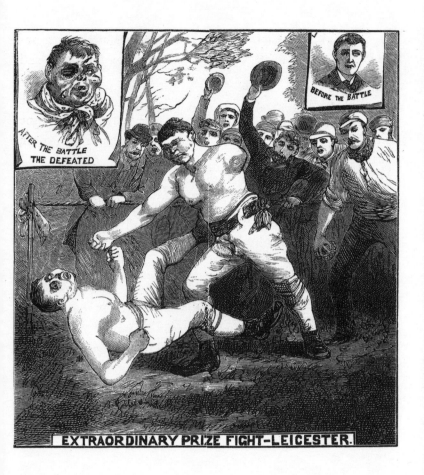

AFTER THE BATTLE
THE DEFEATED

BEFORE THE BATTLE

EXTRAORDINARY PRIZE FIGHT-LEICESTER.

damaged that at last he could not see, and the one-armed man, who was also severely punished, was declared the victor. The stakes were £10. The principals are known to the police.

The Illustrated Police News, May 15, 1886

A Human Skull for a Football

A curious spectacle has been witnessed in a dissenting grave-yard in Heywood this week. A wall in that town, which has for at least two generations served for a fence to the Wesleyan graveyard, was recently blown down, leaving the soil of the graveyard much exposed.

The spot has been used latterly as a playground by children, and on Saturday a number of boys were playing football with what they thought an excellent substitute for a ball.

After diverting themselves for a while, one of the youngsters took hold of the supposed ball, and was terribly frightened on seeing human teeth protruding.

The alarm of the boy attracted a number of men who were working a few yards away, and the substitute for the football was found to be a human skull, which had evidently been washed out of a disturbed grave by the recent heavy rains. It was taken possession of by the proper authorities.

The Manchester Evening News,
November 25, 1882

A Dog in the Football Field

During the match at Aston Lower Grounds on Saturday, between the Aston Villa and West Bromwich Albion, for the Birmingham Cup, an unpleasant incident occurred.

When the game was at its height a tiny white terrier suddenly appeared on the field, and joined in the chase after the ball. He was evidently an enthusiastic devotee of the game. He was very keen on the ball, and had a fine turn of speed on the heavy ground. Wherever the ball went the little terrier followed helter skelter, following every pass, and rushing between the legs of the players to roll over the ball, eagerly biting its smooth sides, while the thousands of spectators roared with merriment and delight. Green captured the dog, and threw it gently on to the heads of the spectators, from whence it scrambled down outside.

It was not to be deprived of its sport that way, for it was soon on the field again. It didn't even appeal to the referee for a foul, but at once joined in the game, and led a wild rush of the Albion forwards for the Villa goal.

It of course greatly hampered the game, and the referee ought to have stopped play until it was removed. At last Burton captured it, and abandoning the game in the kindness of his heart, for the little animal was in constant danger, rushed off with it in his arms towards the dressing-rooms. He had not gone many yards when he met Woodhall coming down the right wing with the ball at his toe. Burton bravely tried to tackle the Albion player with the dog still in his arms, but was at last obliged to drop the dog and devote his undivided attention to Woodhall.

The ball soon went to the Albion backs with doggie after it in full chase, but its football career was over, for one of the Albion backs, meeting it on its way to the ball, gave it a brutal kick, and poor little doggie turned up his legs and lay stiff and still on the damp turf.

Everybody thought it was killed, and the roars of laughter with which the antics of the little fellow had been watched changed into something like a groan of horror, and then into a storm of hisses. Two men ran into the field and carried the dog off, and laid him outside the line of play. There was a cheer all round the ground when at last he wagged his tail.

Supplement to the Leicester Chronicle and Leicestershire Mercury,
March 10, 1888

———

Misconduct of the English Football Players

On Monday evening, a disgraceful scene was witnessed at the Waverley Station, Edinburgh, where the English football players, who took part in the international match, assembled preparatory to leaving the city by the 10.40pm train for the south.

It was evident from the shouting and bawling, and generally boisterous conduct of some of the party, that they had been indulging too freely in strong drink.

The railway officials were unwilling to interfere so long as they confined themselves simply to shouting; but they were forced to do so when one of the Englishmen gave an engine driver a blow on the breast, which sent him reeling against a carriage.

The engine-driver, generously enough, did not press any charge against his assailant, and the players were hustled into a carriage, and the doors locked upon them. Just before the starting of the train, however, one of them got out and struck a railway policeman.

The policeman attempted to detain him, but two of the others, coming to their comrade's assistance, gave the officer some rough treatment.

While the party of four were struggling, the train moved

off, leaving the three Englishmen in the custody of the railway officials who came to the policeman's assistance.

They struggled violently to free themselves, kicking and using their sticks in a savage manner. The policeman received a severe kick while he was lying on the ground, which nearly broke the bridge of his nose.

The prisoners, whose names are Reginald Hasley Burkett, Henry James Graham, and William Gordon, were taken to the Police Office, but were liberated on finding each £2 bail for their re-appearance.

When the case was called in the Police Court, yesterday, Mr Lanton stated that delay for a week had been asked, and as he had no objections Sheriff Hallard agreed to an adjournment. The case will therefore come before the court again next Wednesday.

The Manchester Evening News, March 11, 1875

Amusing Incident at Rock Ferry

Whilst the football match Cheshire Lines v. South Tranmere Y.M.F.S. was in progress last Saturday, a young bullock became very frisky on seeing the players running about in their variegated jerseys.

The bullock rushed in amongst the players, and finally espying Ashton, the Friendlies goalkeeper, between the posts, charged him some distance away, and whilst the goal was left undefended the 'Linesmen' scored a goal, and no whistle being sounded the point was counted.

The Cheshire Observer, October 3, 1891

A Curious Race

In Brooklyn under the auspices of the 'New York World,' a remarkable race recently took place.

The competitors were an elephant, a camel, a horse, a bicycle, and an autocar. The elephant and camel, exhibition animals were ridden by their keepers, the horse was ridden by a famous horseman, and the bicyclist was a sprint rider, and the autocar was driven by an expert.

The elephant and camel were both given a start of half a mile from the autocar, which was given an eighth of a mile by the horse and bicycle, the course being three miles. The elephant proved the victor, winning in 6min. 20sec., with the bicycle second, and the autocar third.

The Midland Daily Telegraph, Coventry, May 22, 1899

Exciting Scene at a Football Match

An extraordinary and exciting scene was witnessed on Christmas afternoon, on the Blackburn Rovers' football ground at Ewood.

The Rovers were advertised to play the Darwen men, and as there has always been a great deal of rivalry between the teams quite 5,000 spectators paid a double admission fee, a large majority of them coming from Darwen.

The sudden thaw of Christmas Eve was followed by a sharp frost, and when the time announced for play arrived the field was literally a sheet of ice, on which it was impossible to walk with safety.

Under these circumstances, the committee of the Rovers, in view of the fact that they had next day to play Wolverhampton Wanderers, sent out their second team. The Darwen players followed on the field, but as soon as the spectators detected the composition of the Rovers' team there were angry shouts from the Darwen supporters, culminating in an uproarious command to their men to retire.

After a consultation, Marsden, the Darwen captain, led his men back to the dressing-room amid tumultuous cheering. After a short pause the Darwen second string appeared on the field, but at this point a mob of spectators got over the barriers, and over-ran the field, finally surrounding the dressing-rooms in a very threatening manner.

The force of police on the ground was very small, and utterly unable to cope with the mob, many of whom were seen to pick up large boulder stones. The squabbling among the 'authorities' of the clubs continued for some time, and then it was announced that the match was abandoned, and that spectators would receive tickets for another match.

A large number availed themselves of this intimation and left the ground, but some 2,000 remained, and after smashing the window of the dressing-room, rushed to the goal posts which they tore down and smashed to fragments. They then invaded the grand stand, and stripping the seats of the carpet covering, carried them into the enclosure, and cut them to shreds.

The huge flag which floated over the entrance gates was also torn down and destroyed. Mr Mark Russell, one of the Rovers' committee, was recognised and savagely assaulted, and a ground man coming to his rescue, received a severe kick on the ankle. Mr T. Eastwood, secretary of the East Lancashire

Cricket Club, was mistaken for an official, and was threatened by a number of roughs, although he explained that he was not connected with the club.

Many other serious cases of assault took place, and it was two hours before the crowd thinned down enough to enable the police to clear the ground and release the besieged officials and players. The gate receipts, which would amount to a very heavy sum, were conveyed to a place of safety as soon as matters looked threatening.

No such scene has been witnessed on the Blackburn Rovers' ground since the memorable occasion, nine years ago, when a dispute between Suter, of the Rovers, and Marshall, of Darwen, caused wild disorder.

The Western Mail, Cardiff, December 29, 1890

Extraordinary Golf Incident

While the members of a Kenilworth Golf Club were playing a mixed four on Saturday a remarkable incident took place.

One of the players, Mr G.W. Hume, made a fine drive, the ball when in mid-air striking a chaffinch and cutting its head completely off. Such an incident as this, it is believed, has never previously happened in connection with the history of the game.

The Daily Mail, Hull, April 13, 1897

✦ INVENTIONS ✦

~ *Preface* ~

James Boyle had a lightbulb moment. A nifty solution to one of the niggles of the age. To that one part inspiration he added the nine parts perspiration the old adage demands, sketched out the technical details and strode off purposefully to make it all official.

The result was US patent number 556248: a saluting hat designed to take the inconvenience out of greeting passing ladies.

Here's how it worked, according to the Middlesbrough *Daily Gazette* of April 1896. 'When the wearer bows the swinging of a pivoted weight block pushes a rod whereby a spring is released and an arm is operated to raise a bow piece to which the edges …' Oh, it tipped itself when you bowed; let's just leave it at that.

Why would you need such a thing? Because a Victorian gentleman was bedevilled by etiquette that required him to tip his hat at each gentlewoman he encountered. Not such a problem at a chap's club; rather draining at a la-di-da do.

'Much valuable energy is utilized in tipping the hat repeatedly and my device will relieve one of it and at once cause the hat to be lifted from the head in a natural manner', said Boyle's patent. Necessity may be the mother of invention, as Agatha Christie sort-of once said, but indolence is its dad.

And if not indolence, then delusion. This may have been a golden age of invention, when scientists, engineers, clergymen and workshop-dabblers delivered breakthrough after breakthrough, but for every Edison, Marconi or Nobel, there were Boyles aplenty. Patents were filed for luminous ghosts to scare off grave-robbers, for ploughs with cannon attachments for blasting crows, for food-graters-cum-fly-traps and for pasteboard cats coated in phosphorous to terrify mice.

There was one for a tapeworm fish hook too. 'That speaks for itself', sniffed the *Derby Daily Telegraph* in March 1890. But in case it doesn't, the uncomfortable details are on page 136.

A Victim to His Own Invention

America is ever supplying us with famous stories, and that of Samuel Wardell, of Flatbush, U.S., ranks amongst the number.

Wardell lived alone. For about two years he had been a lamplighter. In order to get up at five in the morning he was in the habit of putting a 10lb stone on the shelf, connected by a wire with an alarm clock.

When the alarm struck the wire pulled a catch which let the shelf fall, and the stone then fell on the floor with a big thump.

The noise would awaken Wardell, who would jump up and run off to put out the lamps.

On Christmas Eve he invited about 30 young men of the town to supper. As Samuel only had one room in the house, he had removed all his furniture into the cellar. After the company had left he carried back his bedstead into the room, and, being tired, did not pay particular attention where he placed it, and worse than all, forgot all about his clock.

It happened that when he stretched himself on the bed his head was directly under the shelf. When the alarm went off at five o'clock the shelf dropped, and the stone fell on Wardell's head, crushing the skull. He was subsequently discovered by a friend, and was taken to the hospital, where he died.

The Citizen, Gloucester, January 19, 1886

An Eccentric Inventor's Folly

A startling incident occurred at New Bedford on the night of the Presidential election. Mr Patrick Cunningham, one of the richest men in the town, who recently invented an automobile torpedo, which has been adopted by the Government, got very drunk on election night, and declared he would celebrate the event.

He accordingly went to his foundry, selected a section of his torpedo, consisting of an inner and an outer steel shell, conical in shape, loaded with 125lb of slow-burning powder tightly packed, the whole weighing some 500lb, and conveyed it upon a waggon to the corner of two main streets.

Placing the torpedo in the middle of the street he lighted it, and the machine at once started down the street at a terrific pace, flying about 1ft above the surface of the ground.

In its progress the torpedo collided with a tree, and glancing across the street struck the front of the market building sideways. The building at once collapsed.

The torpedo then exploded, shattering several blocks of houses in the vicinity. The report was heard some miles away.

Fortunately no one was killed, but four persons who were in the market-place at the time were thrown violently upon a heap of debris, while others were injured by flying pieces of stone and timber.

A portion of the torpedo, weighing 75lb was found in the adjoining street, having rebounded over the roofs of the intervening houses. Mr Cunningham has been arrested and committed for trial.

The Worcestershire Chronicle, November 14, 1896

A Martyr to Science

The Sicilian tyrant Phalaris was roasted on the instrument he had prepared for the roasting of others, and by a singular fatality a French engineer has just fallen the first victim to his own 'murderous invention.'

The poor fellow lived in the Faubourg St Antoine, and had for a considerable time been engaged in fabricating an engine of war which should sweep away whole columns, and provide his countrymen with an incomparable weapon of vengeance.

He had spent all he possessed on his deadly invention, and had become so absorbed in it and so furious at his repeated failures, that his friends were on the point of putting him under constraint.

On Saturday last they left him making a final experiment. In a few hours, however, an awful explosion was heard; all the windows in the neighbourhood were broken, and volumes of smoke were pouring from the apartment.

The police at once forced an entrance, and found the implement of war burst into pieces, and the inventor himself lying in fragments about the room. He had placed upon his table a hundred leaden soldiers, such as children play with, dressed in the Prussian uniform, loaded his machine to the muzzle with his own composition and missiles, and fired it off. His remains were collected limb by limb and conveyed to the morgue.

The Hampshire Telegraph and Sussex Chronicle,
September 28, 1872

A Wonderful Bed

A Parisian millionaire, M. Lang, has recently had made for him a wonderful bed, which is certainly one of the most luxurious pieces of furniture yet heard of.

When it is time to get up, a chime of bells ring. The occupant continues to sleep. Suddenly a candle is lit by a clever mechanical arrangement. The sleeper rubs his eyes, and an invisible hand proceeds to divest him of his nightcap. By means of electricity a spirit lamp with coffee-roasting apparatus affixed next begins to burn. The water soon boils and the smell of coffee fills the room with a delicious fragrance.

Luxuriously revelling in a crowd of agreeable sensations, the occupant, now just beginning to wake, is soothed by sounds proceeding from a costly musical-box. At length the bells ring out another merry peal, and at the foot of the bed a card with 'Levez-vous' ('Get up') inscribed on it appears. If this invitation is without effect a powerful mechanism lifts the occupant bodily from his bed and deposits him on the floor.

The Worcestershire Chronicle, March 6, 1886

A Steam Man

The *Newark Advertiser* (New Jersey) describes the very extraordinary invention of a machine which moved by steam will perform some of the most important functions of humanity – stand upright, walk or run as he is bid, in any direction, and at almost any rate of speed, drawing after him a load whose weight would tax the strength of three stout draught horses.

In order to prevent the 'giant' from frightening horses by its wonderful appearance, the inventor intends to clothe it, and give it as nearly as possible a likeness to the rest of humanity.

The boilers and such parts as are necessarily heated will be encased in felt or woollen garments. Pantaloons, coat, and vest of the latest styles are provided. Whenever the fires need coaling, which is every two or three hours, the driver stops the machine, descends from his seat, unbuttons 'camel's' vest, opens a door, shovels in the fuel, buttons up the vest, and drives on.

On the back, between the shoulders, the steam cocks and gauges are placed; as these would cause the coat to sit awkwardly, a knapsack has been provided which completely covers them, a blanket neatly rolled up and placed on the top of the knapsack perfects the delusion. The face is moulded into a cheerful countenance of white enamel, which contrasts well with the dark hair and moustache. A sheet-iron hat with a gauge top acts as a smoke stack.

The cost of this 'best man' is $2,000, though its makers expect to manufacture succeeding ones, warranted to run a year without repairs, for $100. The man now constructed can make his way without difficulty over any irregular surface whose ruts and stones are not more than 6 inches below or above the level of the road.

The Taunton Courier, March 18, 1868

———

A Wonderful Invention

The latest Yankee invention is worth hearing about, but whether it will be a nice thing to hear is another matter. It is said that a Troy inventor will shortly take a patent for a cataphone.

As its name implies, the invention has something to do with the noise of the feline race. By means of wires stretched along backyard fences and house tops the inventor conveys, with the aid of some machinery, all concaternated caterwauls into an air-tight barrel.

By another simple contrivance the sounds can be ejected, and can be used in quantities for fire and burglar alarms. The inventor says the instrument is useful for blasting rocks.

The Evening News, Portsmouth, November 4, 1878

A Curious American Invention

The *Hospital*, referring to the issue in the United States of some curious patents in medicine and surgery, says: There is a patent tape-worm trap, consisting of a gold capsule about the shape and size of the gelatine capsules used by pharmacists.

This capsule opens longitudinally and sets with a spring, like an old-fashioned rat-trap, and has a ring at one end, to which a piece of silk thread is to be fastened. The patient is to fast two or three days, and then the trap is set, baited with a bit of cheese, and swallowed, leaving the silk string hanging out of the mouth.

In a few moments it is supposed that the hungry worm will make a dash for the cheese, set free the spring, and leave the jaws of the capsule clasped about his head. Then by means of the string he is to be drawn out hand over hand and coiled away in a bottle, after which you may go fishing for another one.

The Manchester Evening News, October 25, 1890

৩ LIFE and DEATH ৩

Railwayman John Wilkinson died an ironic death. Shortly after clambering into his locomotive, he collapsed, slumping suddenly to the footplate. His workmates dashed to help, but by the time they'd carried him to the waiting room, he'd stopped breathing.

So the train, much like its unfortunate driver, was late that May morning in 1876. But there were few grumbles from the passengers; most of them were dead too.

This minor-key scene played out on the Necropolis Railway, which was built to convey corpses and the bereaved from a dedicated station by Waterloo Bridge to a vast new cemetery in Surrey. It was the largest burial ground in the world at the time, and the most beautiful too, according to an 1888 advert in *The Times* that urged all to visit before making the doleful error of depositing loved ones in 'the seething London cemeteries'.

Therein lies the tale. Crowded beyond compare, the disease-infested boroughs of London had faced a chronic shortage of skeleton space in the first half of the nineteenth century. The canny solution was found in a swathe of land by the village of Brookwood, near Woking, and in the train tracks of the London and South Western Railway.

The first railway funeral was held in November 1854; a truly morose affair for stillborn twin boys from south London. More than 200,000 coffins later, the final passenger to make the one-way trip along the line was a Chelsea pensioner buried in April 1941, shortly before Luftwaffe bombs fell around Waterloo and closed down the operation. In between, there's a good chance poor Mr Wilkinson ended up in the hearse carriages at the back of his own train. Perhaps he knew that day would come, wondering only as to the timing and the cause.

And when it came to causes, there were plenty of contenders for the average Briton: consumption, cholera, smallpox, convulsions, dysentery, dropsy ... With the singles charts a full century away, the *Leicestershire Mercury* began printing a regular countdown of the various ways the townsfolk had died. In the early 1840s, the mortality figures appeared four times a year. By the end of the decade, the table was in each month. By the early 1850s, it was a weekly rundown. Maybe the statistics were being compiled ever faster. Or maybe they proved so popular they just needed to be.

Death fascinated the Victorians, with their grandiose funerals, cult of mourning and keepsake photographs of lifeless loved ones propped up in their Sunday best. And the newspapers of the day indulged them, with reports of calamities and murders that dripped with unpleasant, unnecessary detail.

By contrast, in a topsy-turvy twist to the norm, we are the ones who seem prudish.

A Tragic Story

The tragic circumstances surrounding the death of a well-known Brooklyn doctor named Park are exciting much sympathy. Mrs Park died, as it was supposed and the husband was completely prostrated. As the undertakers were putting Mrs Park into her coffin she revived; the shock to Dr Park, aided by other physical complications, caused his death two hours afterwards.

The Nottingham Evening Post,
January 18, 1890

Laughed Himself to Death

Wesley Parsons, an aged and well-known farmer, died at Laurel, Ind. under peculiar circumstances. While joking with friends he was seized with a spell of laughing, being unable to stop. He laughed for nearly an hour, when he began hiccoughing, and two hours later he died from exhaustion.

The Star, Guernsey, December 14, 1893

Buried Alive

A rich manufacturer, named Oppelt died about 15 years ago at Reichenberg, in Austria, and a vault was built by his widow and children in the cemetery for the reception of the body.

The widow died about a month ago, and was taken to the same tomb; but when it was opened for that purpose, the coffin of her husband was found open and empty, and the skeleton of the deceased discovered in a corner of the vault in a sitting posture.

It is supposed that M. Oppelt was only in a trance when buried, and that on coming to life he had forced open the coffin.

The Worcestershire Chronicle, May 19, 1858

Novel and Fatal Balloon Duel

A deadly encounter between balloonists is reported from Guayana. It appears that M. Molica, a Portuguese gentleman, sent a challenge to a Dutchman, who, according to the rules that are adopted in all cases of this sort, had the choice of weapons and manner of meeting.

The Dutchman, who is an aeronaut, elected to ascend in his balloon; his adversary to adopt a similar course in a balloon borrowed for the occasion. The terms were agreed to, and each belligerent, accompanied by his second, ascended simultaneously.

At a given time the combatants discharged their weapons. M. Molica was wounded slightly, while his antagonist received a mortal wound, from the effects of which he expired in less than two hours. The affair has caused quite a sensation in the locality in which it took place.

The Illustrated Police News, March 16, 1878

NOVEL & FATAL BALLOON DUEL.

Fall Into a Grave.
Sad Death of a Step-Father

Walter W. Fish, an old resident of Rochester, Pennsylvania, was found dead last week in the grave destined for his step-daughter, Mrs William Shell.

Fish had dug the grave and returned home, but was not present at the funeral. When the procession arrived at the cemetery, James Brotherton looked into the grave and saw Mr Fish lying dead in the rough box.

The undertaker, who was on the hearse, was notified, and kept the mourners in the carriages in ignorance of what had occurred. Aided by the pallbearers, Fish's body was removed from the grave and taken away. The funeral then proceeded without the wife of the family knowing the father's fate, until their return home.

At the coroner's inquest it was discovered that Fish's neck was broken. The theory is that he stumbled and fell into the open grave. He was 60 years old.

The Western Mail, Cardiff, December 12, 1893

France

A remarkable case of mistaken identity is reported from Fecamp. The body of a man was found recently in the Rue de Valmont, and after the usual formalities was buried as that of an octogenarian named Godefroy. Two of Godefroy's daughters attended the funeral.

When they returned home they nearly died of terror at finding their father sitting in his usual place near the fire. The shrieks of the women, who thought they saw a ghost, brought in the neighbours, who restored them to consciousness. The error was due to a remarkable likeness between Godefroy and the man who had been found dead.

The Morning Post, November 2, 1896

Killed by a Mouse
Extraordinary Occurrence

An extraordinary occurrence has been brought to light at an inquest of a man in South London. It appears that in a workroom where many young girls were at work a mouse suddenly made its appearance on a table, causing, of course, considerable commotion and a general stampede.

The intruder was seized, however, by a young man who happened to be present, but the mouse slipped out of his hand, and running up his sleeve, came out between his waistcoat and shirt at the neck.

The unfortunate man had his mouth open, and the mouse on the look out for some convenient place of concealment, entered the man's mouth, and he, in his fright and surprise, swallowed it.

That a mouse can exist for a considerable time without much air has long been a popular belief and was unfortunately proved to be a fact in the present instance, for the mouse began to tear and bite inside the man's throat and chest, and the result was that the unfortunate fellow died after a little time in horrible agony.

Several witnesses having corroborated the above facts, and medical testimony as to the cause of death having been given, a verdict of accidental death was returned.

The Manchester Evening News,
December 31, 1875

Singular Affair in London

An extraordinary case of being lost in London, which has resulted in the death of a child scarcely six weeks old, was brought to light this morning.

It would appear that a Mrs Susan Cox had resided for some time past in Elliot's Row, St George's Road, Southwark, with her husband and family.

On Tuesday last the family removed from that address to a house in a turning off the Walworth Road, but so that Mrs Cox should not be worried with the moving, she with her baby, which was six weeks old, went to Bayswater, to remain at the house of a friend.

Mrs Cox stayed there during Tuesday night, but started out at three o'clock yesterday afternoon from her friend's house to her new home, which she had seen previous to the removing, but she was not certain as to the name of the street.

However, she felt sure she could find the place, and took the underground railway to Westminster. From that point she started to walk to her home and got as far as the Elephant and Castle.

According to her own statement she searched for Duke Street (there is no such street in the neighbourhood) thinking that to be the name of the street to which her household had removed; but, after wandering through the neighbourhood for several hours, constantly going over the same ground, she found herself no nearer her destination than when she started.

All her inquiries and searches to find her residence proved futile. During the whole of this time the mother was carrying her baby about with her. As time went on and the shops began to close, Mrs Cox determined to give up the search and find a suitable lodging.

At eleven o'clock last night she found herself near a private hotel in Newington Butts. Here she engaged a room for the night, but she had no sooner sat down than she found that her child was lifeless.

The poor woman seemed completely dazed at the discovery, and it was some time before she could offer any statement. Ultimately a police constable was called in, and it was decided that Mrs Cox should proceed to the Kennington Lane Police Station, where both she and her child were seen by Dr Farr, the divisional surgeon.

The poor woman, however, seemed to have lost her memory, and it was some time before she could give the statement which is detailed above. The body of the child was then conveyed to the Newington mortuary, and after Mrs Cox had made another but futile search for her residence, in company with Sergeant Bontick, she was taken in an exhausted condition to the St Saviour Union Workhouse.

The Manchester Evening News, February 4, 1886

Shocking and Fatal Mistake

A *Dalziel* despatch, dated Jasper (Indiana), Nov 26, states: A farmer named Thomas Atkins, while hunting yesterday, noticed that his dog had tracked something in a hollow tree-trunk. Thinking that he had found a 'catamount,' Atkins called off his dog and shot into the end of the trunk.

He then took a stick and pushed out the object that he had shot. It proved to be the body of his own boy, aged four years, whose head had been completely blown off. Atkins attempted to commit suicide when he found what he had done, but did not succeed.

The Midland Daily Telegraph, Coventry, November 27, 1891

A Peculiar Case

A man named William Hutchinson was recently admitted to the Edinburgh Royal Infirmary, suffering from a pain in the chest, a cough, and shortness of breath. He was treated for heart disease and consumption, but he sank gradually for about a month, when he died.

A post-mortem examination of the body was made, and embedded in the right lung, a musket bullet was found. The deceased, who was 41 years of age, had been a soldier, and served in the Indian Mutiny of 1857–8. He was shot in the right side of the chest, but the wound healed. He subsequently served the remaining portion of his time with his regiment, and was discharged with a pension.

He returned to Edinburgh, where he eked out a livelihood as a hawker for many years, being in no wise troubled with the bullet, which no doubt ultimately caused his death. In fact, until within three months of his death, he enjoyed unbroken health.

The bullet had hollowed out a cavity for itself near the apex of the lung, where it must have rolled about during life. It was encrusted with a hard white substance, and weighed about an ounce and a quarter.

The Edinburgh Evening News, November 9, 1878

Singular Cause of Death

A young lady in Reading, Pa., has just died from sheer fright, produced through a foolish fancy. Having had her photograph taken, she showed a copy to her mother, who discovered the form of a skull on the pictures. Another skull having been figured out, the young lady grew pale, took to her bed, and died.

The Edinburgh Evening News, September 7, 1876

Sudden Death of a Lady From Being Shot at with a Toy Pistol

On Saturday evening, as Mrs Norris, who with her two sisters have for many years kept a haberdasher's and stationer's shop in Brentwood, was serving some customers, some boys threw some peas at the shop window and into the shop.

She ran to the door to drive them away, when one of them fired a toy pistol at her. She instantly dropped down dead. She had previously been suffering from a slight affection of the heart.

The Grantham Journal, January 30, 1869

Strange Death of a Professor

A retired University professor, M. Louis Gerard, aged 56, met with a singular and terrible death, on Friday night, at Paris.

A match he had struck to light his pipe set fire to his long and bushy beard. It flared up tremendously and the flames caught his hair, and then set fire to his clothes.

Before they could be extinguished, the unfortunate gentleman had been so shockingly burned that he died from exhaustion half an hour later.

The Cornishman, March 2, 1899

A Mexican Chapter of Horrors

A correspondent of the *Morning Post*, writing from Mexico on the 29th ult., says: One of the female scholars in one of the public schools of the city the other day found at home a packet of strychnia, and quite ignorant of the fatal properties of the drug, she brought it to the school house and placed it in the vessel containing the water for the use of her fellow-pupils.

Eight of them drank the poisoned water, and four of them, including the author of the calamity, expired in great agony.

The Dundee Courier and Argus,
December 10, 1868

Killed by a Coffin

Dr Lankester held an inquest on Saturday evening at the University College Hospital on the body of Henry Taylor, aged sixty-six.

The evidence of Mr E.J. Reading, an undertaker's foreman, and others, showed that on the 19th instant the deceased, with others, was engaged at a funeral at Kensal Green Cemetery.

The church service having been finished, the coffin and mourners proceeded in coaches towards the place of burial. The day being damp, the foreman directed the coaches with the mourners to proceed to the grave by the footway, and the hearse across the grass towards a grave-digger, who was motioning the nearest way.

The coffin was moved from the hearse and being carried down a path only three feet wide, by six bearers, when orders were given to turn, so that the coffin, which was what is known in the trade as a 4lb leaden one, should go head first.

While the men were changing, it is supposed that the deceased caught his foot against a sidestone and stumbled; the other bearers, to save themselves, let the coffin go, and it fell with great force on to the deceased, fracturing his jaws and ribs.

The greatest confusion was created amongst the mourners who witnessed the accident, and the widow of the person about to be buried nearly went into hysterics.

Further assistance having been procured, the burial service was proceeded with, while the deceased was conveyed to a surgery, and ultimately to the above-mentioned hospital, where he expired on the 24th instant.

KILLED BY A COFFIN AT KENSAL GREEN CEMETERY.

The jury recommended that straps should be placed round coffins, which would tend to prevent such accidents. Verdict – accidental death.

The Illustrated Police News,
November 2, 1872

Choked by a Billiard Ball

A singular death occurred on Wednesday night at a public house in Soho, London. Some men were in the billiard room, when one of them attempted to get a billiard ball into his mouth. This feat he had previously accomplished, and had successfully removed the ball.

This time, however, he failed to extract it, and it became fixed in his throat. A cab was immediately fetched, but while being removed to the hospital the unfortunate fellow expired.

The Sheffield and Rotherham Independent,
November 4, 1893

Awful Occurence

On Monday morning last, a woman named Jones, at Mullahead, near Tandragee, went out of the house, leaving her two children in the kitchen with a pot of water ready for scalding the churn.

The children began to play hide and seek, and one of them got into the churn and put on the lid. The mother came in, and in a hurry threw in the water and scalded the child to death. The other called out to her what she had done, when she took up a stool and dashed out its brains, and then ran out and is supposed to have drowned herself as she has not yet been discovered.

The Cork Examiner, March 20, 1843

Missing for Four Months and Dead at Home at Last

The American newspapers report a curious case. A man named Colt, living in New York, disappeared on the second of December last, being last seen by the conductor of a car apparently going towards his home. The relatives and his wife made every exertion to find Colt, without the slightest success.

About the time her husband disappeared, Mrs Colt noticed that the outhouse door, which fastened with a spring lock, was shut, and as she had no key, she was unable to open it. The natural grief and anxiety attending the fruitless search for her missing husband, caused Mrs Colt to pay no special heed to the circumstance, and she made no effort to open the door.

Mr Colt still continuing to be missing, his wife and children were finally compelled after an interval of some three weeks, to leave their residence and seek another more suited to their changed circumstances. The second floor which they had occupied was not re-let and still remains untenanted.

On Tuesday, several boys residing in the neighbourhood engaged in a game at 'hide and seek,' and one of them in the course of his play peered through a knot-hole in the side of the outhouse already spoken of, and was surprised to see the form of a man therein.

The police were subsequently notified, and broke open the door, and discovered that the man was quite dead and slightly black in the face. It proved to be the missing Colt. The process of decomposition had in some unexplained manner been greatly retarded.

The Grantham Journal,
May 7, 1870

A Strange Discovery

A box was sent from Tynemouth to Canterbury a fortnight ago, but the person to whom it was addressed could not be found. The box has just been opened, and the dead body of a child found in it.

The Sunderland Daily Echo and Shipping Gazette,
January 22, 1886

Lost in a Fog.
Twenty Persons Drowned

A fog of extraordinary density prevailed at Amsterdam, on Thursday night, compelling the suspension of vehicular traffic and rendering it highly dangerous for pedestrians to make their way from one part of the city to another.

It is stated this morning that no fewer than seventy-nine persons, who were out last night, missed their way and fell into the water of the various canals which intersect the city. Of these twenty at least were drowned, while several others are still missing.

The Evening News, Portsmouth, December 30, 1893

An Incident of the Influenza

A peculiar incident is reported from Strood-next-Rochester. An elderly lady died from influenza, and the funeral was to have taken place a week ago. On the day appointed for the interment, however, all the mourners were down with the same malady, and the body was consequently removed to the mortuary.

Since then the deceased's two sisters, who had resided with her, have died from influenza, and a sister-in-law is lying dangerously ill. A triple funeral will take place to-day.

The Devon and Exeter Daily Gazette, March 14, 1895

Born in a Grave

A Vienna correspondent telegraphs: The *Pester Lloyd* reports a horrible story from a village near Szegedin, in Hungary.

The wife of a landed proprietor, Michael Gouda, died before giving birth to a child. The village doctor confirmed her death, and she was buried. Three days afterwards the husband began to entertain doubts as to the certainty of her death, and would not rest until the police had caused his wife to be exhumed.

The body was found lying on one side, and when the clothes were removed the corpse of a new-born child was found lying beside its mother. The local doctors assert that the child was born from the dead woman, but in Budapest it is believed that she was buried alive in a cataleptic condition. The husband is frantic.

The Evening News, Portsmouth, September 20, 1890

Delicacy and Drowning

The *Hampshire Telegraph*, in its 'Naval Section,' relates the following curious story from Bermuda: 'A party of blue-jackets were returning from Hamilton by steamboat, having just been on general leave, when a quarrel took place. According to my information one of the parties to this quarrel struck the man with whom he was contending, the result being that the latter went overboard.

'A marine, having observed what had taken place, immediately peeled to jump in; but as he was just dropping the last article of attire and preparing for his spring, an officer ordered him to dress, as there were ladies in a boat close by.

'A life-buoy was thrown overboard, and the ladies in the boat manifested every description of sympathy with the unfortunate man, who was now some two or three hundred yards astern, but seemed altogether opposed to the idea of an ordinary man springing into the sea unless duly and sufficiently attired in the garments which fashion rather than common sense has decided to be proper.

'A sudden sweep of the boat brought the position of the unfortunate swimmer into view, and his frantic efforts to keep afloat at last created in the minds of those who were watching some idea of his imminent danger. Now the officer thought it necessary to ask if anyone could swim, and hardly were the words uttered when over went five men to the rescue, including the marine.

'The action taken, however, was too late, and the poor fellow sank and was drowned. From this moment it seemed to occur to this young officer that he had been guilty of, to put it mildly, an act of false delicacy interwoven with a spice of inhumanity. Boats were now sent out and everything done that should have been done very much earlier. A coroner's jury has assembled, and a verdict of "Found drowned" has been returned.'

The Western Daily Press, Bristol, June 9, 1892

The Dead Sailor and His Dog.
A Terrible Discovery

A most extraordinary discovery was made a few weeks ago by two sailors belonging to a vessel named the Prairie Queen.

The mariners in question landed on one of the cluster of small islands in the Indian Ocean known as the Maldives. Most of these are uninhabited. They are situated south-west of Cape Comorin. The sailors' leave of absence did not extend beyond the brief space of two hours.

In less than half that time they came upon an object the sight of which transfixed them in a state of speechless astonishment and horror. They observed the ghastly remains of a human being hanging across the branch of a tree which one hand of the figure still grasped.

At their approach a flock of vultures flew off in all directions. The figure was nearly reduced to a mere skeleton, but the remnants of garments that partially clothed it served to show that the dead man was either an English or an American sailor. This was more clearly demonstrated upon closer inspection. On a branch of the tree the following name and date were carved –

S. PARKER. 1872

Near to the tree and its ghastly burden was a retriever dog, the howlings of which had attracted the sailors to the spot. They forthwith induced the captain and crew to witness the sad spectacle, and the general impression on the minds of all on board the Prairie Queen was that the strange figure was all that remained of a ship-wrecked sailor, who had sought the island in question as a haven of rest, and found thereon a grave.

Whether the ill-fated man died from want and exposure, or from the effects of lightning, or a sunstroke, it is not possible to say. The dog was doubtless saved with him from the wreck. How the poor animal managed to find food can be

THE DEAD SAILOR AND HIS DOG

readily understood. The two sailors, before they left the island, dug a shallow grave, in which they deposited the remains. The dog they took with them and the faithful creature soon became a great favourite with every man and boy on board the Prairie Queen.

The Illustrated Police News, January 3, 1874

A Strange Will

A well-known citizen of Brooklyn, U.S., alike renowned for his wealth and eccentricity, died a few weeks ago, and his last will and testament was found by his sorrowing relatives with whom he had been at odds during his life, to contain the following curious bequests: 'I own seventy-one pairs of trousers. It is my desire that they be sold by public auction after my death, and that the product of their sale be distributed among the deserving poor of my parish. They must, however, be disposed of severally to different bidders, no single individual being permitted to purchase more than one pair.'

These directions were duly carried out by the heirs-at-law. The seventy-one pairs of trousers were successively knocked down to seventy-one purchasers, and their price was handed over to the parochial authorities.

A few days after the sale one of the buyers took it into his head to make a careful examination of his newly-acquired property, and found a small canvas bag neatly sewn up in the waistband. Upon opening this bag an agreeable surprise met his gaze, in the shape of ten one hundred dollar notes.

The tidings of this amazing discovery spread like wildfire throughout Brooklyn and New York, and each fortunate possessor of a pair of these precious pantaloons was rejoiced to find his investigations rewarded by the acquisition of a sum equivalent to two hundred pounds sterling.

It seems that the eccentric testator's heirs have instituted proceedings to recover the amounts secreted by him in the linings of his trousers from the present proprietors of those garments, on the ground that he was obviously out of his mind when he made such an insensate will.

The Star, Guernsey, February 24, 1880

An Extraordinary Will

A cabman has committed suicide in Paris in a fit of disgust at things in general. In his pocket he left a most singular will. It directs that in the left pocket of his trousers will be found a ten-franc piece, which is to be given to the doctor who signs the certificate of his death. The body is to be carried to the Jardin des Plantes and dissected. The flesh is to be cut into slices and divided among the lions, tiger, and bears. The testator adds, 'I intend that these animals shall regale themselves upon my flesh.'

The Western Daily Press, Bristol,
August 23, 1888

The Astonished Photographer

A well-known artist of the camera, says the London correspondent of the *Sheffield Daily Telegraph*, was lately called in to
photograph the body of a young lady who had just 'died' under
peculiar and distressing circumstances.

The body was laid out on the sofa in the drawing-room. The
photographer, who was left alone in the room with the body,
took a negative. After inspecting it, he took another. And then,
to his amazement, he discovered that the two negatives were
not alike. The body must have moved!

He instantly summoned the nurse and a doctor, when it was
ascertained that the poor girl had never departed this life. Her
sleep had been only that of a trance.

The Hull Daily Mail, March 19, 1889

Incredible Carelessness

A tragic occurrence is reported from Widnes. On Saturday
night, a youth named Hague was sent by his master, a wholesale
draper named Birchall, to his lodgings for a four-chambered
revolver, which the master intended presenting to a policeman
going to Australia.

At the lodgings Hague shot himself through the mouth with
the revolver, it is supposed while inspecting it. The domestic servant was showing a neighbour how it occurred, when the firearm
again went off, and shot her through the mouth. Both are dead.

The Sunderland Daily Echo and Shipping Gazette,
October 10, 1881

Strange Attempt at Suicide

On Thursday morning a strange attempt at suicide was made by a gentleman named Isaac House, aged sixty-five years, residing at No. 16, The Grove, Stockwell Green.

About nine o'clock he went up to his bedroom, and having procured a toy cannon, loaded it with powder, placed it on the dressing table, and procured a match. He then stooped down, placed his mouth over the muzzle, and with his right hand fired the cannon. Mrs House, hearing a heavy fall, rushed upstairs and found her husband bleeding.

Assistance was procured, and Mr House was immediately removed to St Thomas's Hospital, and attended by the surgical officials, who found the roof and other portions of the mouth frightfully lacerated, having no less than sixteen irregular gashes. These were successfully stitched up, but in consequence of not being able to stop the haemorrhage, little hopes are entertained of Mr House's recovery.

The Western Daily Press, Bristol, January 1, 1876

Fearful Scene – Women Torn to Pieces by Cats

A report of a dreadful scene has reached us from Javat. It appears that a lady who is as rich as she is eccentric has for the last three or four years become a sort of cat fancier, she not only breeds these domestic pets, but has been accustomed to purchase any choice specimen of the feline race that might take her fancy.

FEARFUL SCENE.—WOMEN TORN TO PIECES BY CATS

A few weeks ago a fire broke out at the house of the cat fancier. Two maid servants were dispatched to a sort of shed or cage on the basement of the premises to unlock the door of the same, and release the cats. The devouring element was by this time in the ascendant, and the cats were in a state bordering on madness.

The moment the door was unlocked, they flew at the unfortunate young women, whom they bit and tore most unmercifully. The injuries were of such a nature that both have died there from.

The Illustrated Police News, July 22, 1876

A School Teacher's Suicide

Miss Cora Brummer, teacher in a public school at Napoleon, in Cincinnati, committed suicide yesterday in an extraordinary fashion.

She asked her pupils for a pocket knife, and having obtained one, stood on the platform in the class-room, and in the presence of them all deliberately cut her throat, inflicting two frightful gashes, death ensuing shortly afterwards.

The reason assigned is that the summer vacation was about to begin, and that she saw no means of living after her salary was exhausted.

The Nottingham Evening Post, June 10, 1895

Killed by a Drunken Bear

A strange and terrible accident has just occurred in the neighbourhood of Vilna, in Russia. A few days ago, a large tame bear, which had been trained by the servants of a country gentleman to drink votky (whiskey), entered a village tavern, and killed the tavern keeper and three members of his family in a fit of intoxication.

The tragedy was brought about by the owner of the tavern, Isaack Rabbanovitch, attempting to snatch from the bear a keg of votky, which it had commenced to drink, after staving it in with its paws. In the conflict that ensued the infuriated animal hugged to death the tavern keeper, his two sons, and daughter.

When the peasants arrived on the scene with guns they found the intoxicated animal asleep on the floor in a pool of blood and votky, surrounded by its four victims. The bear was immediately shot.

The Nottingham Evening Post, August 27, 1891

SUPERSTITION, BELIEF
and the SUPERNATURAL

~ *Preface* ~

Bear-Bind Cottage was a lonely spot. An isolated house on a lane that slunk away from the village of Bow to the huddle of homes at Old Ford and the marshland beyond. The sort of track you might take as a shortcut on a bitter winter's night, then swiftly change your mind and double back.

It was here, at this solitary stretch of nothing in particular, long since swallowed by the East End of London, that eighteen-year-old Jane Alsop was disturbed by the urgent ringing of a bell at the gate on a February evening in 1838.

Outside in the gloom stood a cloaked figure who said he was a policeman and demanded she bring a light. The instant she obliged, he threw off his cape, breathed a fireball of blue and white flame and mauled her with metallic claws until her sister came to the rescue.

Her hair was torn; her dress was ripped: poor Jane had joined a small but growing band of victims of the demon who lurked in the dark corners of the Victorian imagination to the end of the century.

At first the papers had called him Steel Jack, dismissing him as nothing more than an upper-class prankster with particularly bouncy shoes and a wager to settle.

But sightings spread, rumours grew and descriptions became ever more outlandish. His eyes were balls of fire, they said. And he could leap higher than a hedge-row. No! A mail coach. By the time of the attack in Bear-Binder Lane, the press had settled on the name that parents would invoke to disobedient children for decades to come: Spring-Heeled Jack, a devilish mix of Freddy Krueger, Zebedee and Batman gone bad.

Scratch the surface of the age of science and Victorian Britain was riddled with superstition. A century that perfected the art of the ghost story saw parlours resounding with the moans of mediums and the rat-a-tat-tats of the dead. Far from the cities, a lingering belief in witchcraft saw a succession of blameless old ladies being blooded to break a spell. And every now and again there were one-off flare-ups of the heebie-jeebies. In 1842, to the withering scorn of journalists, Londoners abandoned their city in droves, fearing the onset of an earthquake prophesied by the astrologer John Dee in 1598. Almost four decades later, a girl worried herself to death at the fabricated predictions of sixteenth-century soothsayer Mother Shipton, which said the world would end in 1881.

Yet these were mere sideshows compared to the supernatural belief that dominated the Victorian era, even in the face of a rising tide of secularism. It went something like this: 1. There is a God. 2. He's probably British. 3. On the whole, it's not seemly to get too excitable about such matters.

Lynching a Ghost

A remarkable instance of superstition is, the St Petersburg correspondent of the *Daily Graphic* says, reported from Orenburg.

During the funeral of a wealthy peasant the lid of the coffin was seen to rise, and the corpse proceed to get out. The priest and mourners were so alarmed that they ran back to their village, and locked themselves up in their huts.

The corpse, who was feeling cold (as corpses should), ran after them, and succeeded in getting into the hut of an aged peasant woman, who had not been quite so agile as the rest in fastening the door.

The peasants, when they had recovered from their panic and learned where the corpse was, proceeded with guns and stakes of pine to 'exorcise' the 'ghost,' and killed him.

When the priest had sufficiently collected his senses to explain the phenomenon of the ghost by the hypothesis of a prolonged stated of coma, and came out of his hut to rescue him, he found that the peasants, having 'laid' the ghost, had thrown him into a marshy field.

The Citizen, Gloucester, March 12, 1890

A Strange Story

A *Press Association* despatch says: Adelaide Amy Terry, servant to Dr Williams, of Brentford, was sent to a neighbour with a message on Sunday evening, and as she did not return and was known to be short-sighted, it was feared she had fallen into the canal, which was dragged, but without success.

On Tuesday an old barge-woman suggested that a loaf of bread in which some quicksilver had been placed should be floated in the water. This was done, and the loaf became stationary at a certain spot. The dragging was resumed there, and the body was discovered.

The Tamworth Herald, October 27, 1883

A Ghost at Wrexham

For some time the inhabitants of Wrexham have been kept in a state of excitement by rumours that 'a ghost' was to be seen in the neighbourhood of Salisbury Park. Most determined efforts have been made to capture the nocturnal visitor, but he or she has hitherto managed to escape.

A strict watch has, however, been kept, and the assemblage of idlers and roughs congregated to wait for the ghost have of late become a serious nuisance, as, in default of having a ghost to look after, they have amused themselves by insulting casual passers by.

On Saturday night the crowd discovered a 'something' which they were pleased to call the ghost in Salisbury Park. A rush was made at once for the supposed apparition, stones were thrown and dogs were slipped at the unfortunate 'ghost,' who ultimately turned out to be an inebriated workman who had, in his drunken confusion wandered through the park.

He was handed over to the police, by whom he was brought before the magistrates yesterday, and was discharged.

The Manchester Evening News, September 22, 1874

A Headless Ghost

Superstition rarely stands in the way of the extension of postal accommodation or convenience; but a case of the kind which recently occurred in the west of Ireland is mentioned by the Postmaster-General in his report issued yesterday.

Application was made for the erection of a wall letter-box, and authority had been granted for setting it up; but when arrangements came to be made for providing for the collection of letters, no one could be found to undertake the duty, in consequence of a general belief among the poorer people in the neighbourhood that, at that particular spot, 'a ghost went out nightly on parade.'

The ghost was stated to be a large white turkey without a head.

The Edinburgh Evening News, September 7, 1876

Remarkable Dereliction of Duty

There are some very wicked people in the commune of Châtre-Langlin, in the canton of Saint-Benoit-du-Sault.

At the end of last July a terrible hailstorm occurred there, which did a vast deal of damage. The inhabitants, having arrived at the conviction that their *curé*, if he were good for anything, might have caused the storm to cease by performing certain religious rites, and being very angry with him for not doing so, went in a body to the church and fell upon him. He fled into the sacristy.

They went to his house, pitched his clothes over the window, beat the domestics who tried to interfere, and declared that they meant to 'kill the *curé* because he had let them be hailed upon.' Nothing more irreverent could occur to the African who thrashes his wooden god if it does not bring him rain.

Moreover, the peasants allowed their vengeance to attack persons who could not possibly have anything to do with a hailstorm.

A municipal councillor, we should imagine, would be the last man in the world to trifle with a thunder-cloud, like Benjamin Franklin; but so blind was the wrath of the villagers that they caught and smote severely an official of that description, who had merely endeavoured to rescue the *curé*.

For this offence fourteen persons were last week summoned to appear before a Correctional Tribunal.

The Hampshire Telegraph and Sussex Chronicle,
September 28, 1872

Weird Tragedy in Paris

One of the weirdest tragedies that has occurred for a long time has just taken place in a house in the Rue de Chezy at Neuilly, Paris.

The house was occupied by a widow named Devezins, with her son Frederick and her niece Mlle. Marthe Contresty, who were engaged to be married, and were deeply in love with each other.

Affianced last November they were to be married in the second week of February, but in the middle of January M. Frederick

Devezins fell suddenly ill. He died on January 23 at eleven o'clock at night. His *fiancée* was at his bedside until the end.

Madame Devezins cared for her niece's reason, and sent her to stay with some friends, but to all attempts to raise her spirits she replied: 'Before leaving me my *fiancé* promised not to abandon me. A few minutes before dying, while he still had all his reason, he said: "Do not cry, darling. We will be united in spite of all. I will come for you in a month. Wait on me in your bed-room at the same hour at which I die. I will carry you away, and we will be united in eternity."'

In order not to grieve Madame Devezins the friends did not tell her of her niece's conviction, to which, moreover, little importance was attached.

On Monday, the 19th, Mlle. Contresty, who seemed to have recovered her self-possession, returned to live with her aunt. On Friday, the 23rd, one month after the death of her *fiancé*, she was more dejected than usual, and hardly left her room all day.

After going to bed about eleven o'clock at night Madame Devezins went to see how her niece was. She stopped in amazement at the bed-room door, which was open. Her niece had not heard her approach, and was sitting in an armchair gazing fixedly at the clock. She was wearing the dress in which she was affianced and also her engagement ring. It was almost eleven o'clock. Suddenly the wind blew open the badly-closed window and extinguished the lamp.

Madame Devezins approached her niece, and touched her lightly on the shoulder. Before she could speak there was a scream, and Mlle. Contresty fell to the floor. When help arrived she was found to be dead, a physician who was called explaining that she had died of terror.

The Morning Post, March 1, 1900

An Extraordinary Superstition

At the Bootle Police Court on Monday, before Alderman E. Neep and J. Howard, Mary Ann Proudly, of 10, Aber Street, Bootle, was charged with cruelly treating a cat by cutting off its tail.

Inspector Herniman, of the Royal Society for the Prevention of Cruelty to Animals, supported the prosecution. Mrs Fletcher, of 10, Aber Street, said that on New Year's Day, about five o'clock, the defendant borrowed a hatchet from her. The witness saw her go into her room and deliberately chop the cat's tail off. Next morning the defendant told her that she had cut the cat's tail off to prevent the cat from going mad.

Alderman Howard: And is that the way to cure anybody going mad? (Laughter.) Defendant: Yes, sir, it was going mad with its tail. Alderman Neep: Why didn't you cut the head off instead of the tail, and cure the madness? Defendant: There is a worm in a cat's tail that goes up into its brain and drives it mad. (Laughter.) Alderman Neep: That is something new to me. (Laughter.) Defendant: It never ran after its tail after that. (Loud laughter.) It was quite quiet after that, and I used to give it bread and milk. I only tried to cure the cat from going mad.

Alderman Neep: The sooner it is known that cutting off a cat's tail will not cure madness the better. It is simply nonsense to raise a defence like that. It will be a warning to you, and you will have to pay a fine of 40s. and costs, or go to gaol for a month.

The Lancaster Gazette, January 16, 1889

A Strange Story

An extraordinary story is reported from Prussian Poland. It appears that among the Poles and Hungarians the myth of vampires still finds credence.

A country squire at Roslasin, in Posen, died some months ago, his death being speedily followed by that of his eldest son and the dangerous illness of several of his relatives, all which cases occurred as suddenly as they seemed unaccountable.

The deceased was at once suspected of being a vampire, rising from his grave, and sucking the blood of his surviving friends.

To prevent further mischief his second son determined to chop off the corpse's head, for which enterprise he obtained the assistance of some equally superstitious peasants at a very high price.

The head was to be laid with the feet, while an assistant collected the blood dropping from the neck in a vessel to give to the relatives to drink. The deed was delayed by the interference of the parish priest, but was in the end effected at night, not, however, without an unasked witness.

The case is now before the Prussian Court of Appeals. The local court had sentenced the desecrators of the churchyard to three months imprisonment, and it seems likely that they will still have to pay that penalty for their superstition.

The Manchester Evening News,
May 23, 1871

Superstition in Hungary

A strange story of superstition is reported from Homolitz, in Hungary. Several bodies of men had recently been found there with their heads cut off.

An investigation was made by the police, and it turned out that these mutilations had in every instance been committed by young men who were betrothed to the widows of the decapitated persons.

The husbands had died a natural death, and their widows believed that in case they married a second time their husbands would reappear and destroy their wedded happiness. Hence they had persuaded their new bridegrooms to decapitate their deceased partners.

The Huddersfield Daily Chronicle, April 20, 1892

The Ancient Druids.
Attempt to Burn a Child's Body

The Press Association's Pontypridd correspondent telegraphs that an extraordinary sensation has been caused in Pontypridd and district by the arrest of Dr Price, a surgeon of some considerable celebrity in Glamorganshire and other Welsh counties.

It is stated that an infant child of his housekeeper died in Dr Price's house, and he was seen last night to carry the child's body towards an adjacent hill top, with the apparent intention of burning it according to the rites of the Ancient Druids, in which he is a believer, and for the purpose he had obtained an empty tar barrel.

He was followed, however, by a crowd, who, but for the intervention of the police, would have severely dealt with the doctor. An investigation is now being held into the circumstances attending the child's death. Dr Price was brought before the Pontypridd magistrates this morning, and admitted to bail until Wednesday next.

The Sunderland Daily Echo and Shipping Gazette,
January 15, 1884

Superstition in England

In the recent case at Hedingham – that Mecca of Eastern Counties Toryism – the people have advanced a step even beyond pig-roasting.

There has been a deaf and dumb man there for years, believed, we suppose on some sort of evidence, to be a Frenchman. He does not seem to have been peculiarly obnoxious, for, in spite of his infirmity, he was just before his death dancing with the villagers in the tap-room of the local public house.

Emma Smith, however, grade unknown, but well to do in the world, fell ill, had pains which she could not account for, felt unearthly aches, and, in short, had a touch of the nervous fever, not uncommon in half-drained villages. She attributed it to 'Dummy,' the only name borne by her unfortunate victim.

Accordingly she sought him in the tap-room, and offered him three sovereigns to unbewitch her. The poor wretch, understanding nothing of the matter declined the money, and then two men, Samuel Stammers, builder, and George Gibson, bricklayer, tried to compel him to kiss her, judging, apparently, with a quaint confusion between Christianity and Paganism, that the 'kiss of peace' would undo the evil wrought by witchcraft.

The poor dumb wretch still did not understand, whereupon he was seized by Mrs Smith, dragged to the brook, and ducked repeatedly. Emerging, he was again offered the £3, but, 'dazed' with the assault and the cold water, he only sat himself down on a heap of stones.

The woman seems to have interpreted this into persistent wizard malignity, beat him over the head with a stick, and then plunged him in the stream again, beating his head on the stones.

Her assistant in the good work, Stammers, seems by this time to have been alarmed, and the wretched dumb man, who was even then ill of a lung disease, was allowed to crawl home.

Utterly bewildered and miserable, he crept on to his bed, dressed as he was in his dripping clothes, and next day was found dying of acute inflammation of the lungs. He was conveyed to the Union Infirmary, and so died, ignorant, of course, to the last of the possibility of having given offence. A more horrible case of cruelty never was recorded.

The coroner's jury, nevertheless, could not come to a decision. They argued for two hours – about Stammers' guilt only, says the local reporter, but that must be an error – and were at length discharged without a verdict, and the case referred to the Hedingham bench of magistrates.

They will probably do justice, for the belief in black magic, as we have said, now annoys the upper class; but all the incidents, the belief in the supernatural power of an old dumb Frenchman over his acquaintance, the lavish offering to propitiate his malice, the trust in a compulsory kiss, the savage and protracted cruelty displayed to a wizard to whom the assailant was still offering sacrifice, and the jury too puzzled to know if a death of the kind involved manslaughter, make up a picture which may, perhaps, lower for an hour the tone of our habitual paeans over English humanity and civilisation. What could Africans do worse to propitiate a fetish?

The Dundee Advertiser,
September 25, 1863

Singular Superstition

At Willenhall, yesterday, two young men, brothers, named Green, were charged with assaulting an elderly woman named Roberts. The elder brother admitted striking the woman on the nose, and said he did to draw her blood, she having threatened to bewitch him.

His mother died lately, and he believed the complainant had killed her by witchcraft. The magistrates characterised the assault as cowardly, and fined the prisoners 40s and costs, or two months.

The Edinburgh Evening News,
June 4, 1878

The Earthquake Prophecy

The prophesised earthquake, which was to have come off on Wednesday last, and have demolished St Paul's Cathedral, and the neighbourhood for miles around, disappointed the credulous Irish in the regions of St Giles's.

The *Standard* says that the scene witnessed in the neighbourhoods of St Giles's and Seven Dials during the whole of the day was perhaps the most singular that has presented itself for many years.

Many of the Irish resident in those localities have left for the shores of the Emerald Isle, but by far the larger number, unblessed by the world's goods, have been compelled to remain where they are, and to anticipate the fearful event which was to engulf them in the bowels of the earth.

The frantic cries, the incessant appeals to Heaven for deliverance, the invocations to the Virgin and saints for mediation, the heart-rending supplications for assistance, heard on every side during the day, sufficiently evidenced the power with which this popular delusion had seized the minds of those superstitious people.

Towards the close of the day a large number of them determined not to remain in London during the night, and with what few things they possessed took their departure for what they considered more favoured spots. Some violent contests arose between the believers and the sceptics – contests which in not a few cases were productive of serious results.

The poor Irish, however, are not the only persons who have been credulous in this matter: many persons, from whom better things might have been expected, were amongst the number who left London to avoid the threatened catastrophe.

To the Gravesend steam-boat companies the 'earthquake' proved a source of immense gain; and the same may be said with regard to the various railways. Long before the hour appointed for the starting of steam-boats from London Bridge Wharf, Hungerford Market, and other places, the shore was thronged by crowds of decently-attired people of both sexes, and, in many instances whole families were to be seen with an amount of eatables and drinkables which would have led one to suppose that they were going a six weeks' voyage.

About eleven o'clock the Planet came alongside the London Bridge Wharf, and the rush to get on board of her was tremendous, and in a few minutes there was scarcely standing room on board. The trains on the various railways were, throughout the whole of Tuesday and Wednesday morning, unusually busy in conveying passengers without the prescribed limits of the metropolitan disaster.

To those who had not the means of taking trips to Gravesend or by railway, other places which were supposed to be exempted from the influence of the 'rude commotion' about to take place, were resorted to. From an early hour in the morning, the humbler classes from the east end of the metropolis, sought refuge in the fields beyond the purlieus of Stepney.

On the north, Hampstead and Highgate were favoured with a visit from large bodies of the respectable inhabitants of St Giles's and Primrose Hill also was selected as a famous spot for viewing the demolition of the leviathan city.

The darkness of the day and the thickness of the atmosphere, however, prevented it being seen.

The Westmorland Gazette and Kendal Advertiser,
March 26, 1842

A Dangerous Witch

A lady residing near Blois, in France, has just fallen a victim to her avarice and belief in supernatural agencies combined, and has paid dearly enough for her folly to induce her, one would think, to renounce intercourse with wise women in future.

She possessed a considerable fortune but wanted to increase her riches, and for this purpose consulted a sorceress. The latter went to her residence, conferred with some invisible assistants, by whose advice the lady was told to place all her money in a certain drawer, not to open it for a given time, or the charm would be broken, and before retiring to rest to throw a marvellous white powder into the fire. If these conditions were carried out, the fortune, she was told, would be doubled.

They were carried out, but the result was a distinct deception for the credulous believer in the supernatural. Whilst she abstained from opening the drawer the sorceress emptied it at leisure, and when she threw the white powder into the fire a terrible explosion ensued, she was severely injured, and the house set fire to.

It is satisfactory to know that this dangerous witch has been taken into custody.

The Sunderland Daily Echo and Shipping Gazette,
August 14, 1884

A Curious Superstition

At Brazcka, in Bosnia, an old superstition has come to life again which resembles the fables of Jewish ritual murders.

In Bosnia the people have believed at all times that a bridge could not be firm and lasting unless a human being was walled up in it. Thus there is a legend connected with the handsome Roman bridge at Mostar, which says that the fine arch across the Narenta could not be finished until the architect walled up in it a bridal pair.

Now that a solid bridge is being built across the Save at Brazcka, this superstition is revived. It is rumoured everywhere that gipsies are stealing children to sell them to the contractors, who wall one up in each pillar.

The Yorkshire Evening Post, August 12, 1893

Singular Superstition: Laying a Ghost

A Newhaven despatch to a New York paper says: In the Roman Catholic Cemetery in Birmingham, early on the morning of the 18th ult., four middle-aged women and two men, the latter armed with spades and picks, entered by the side gate and halted in front of a newly-made grave.

The men set to work, while the women wept, and opened the grave and hauled a coffin up. The lid was taken off, and the remains of a beautiful young girl were revealed. She was the daughter of one of the women, and the mother shrieked loudly when she saw the corpse.

The men stood aside and the four women bent over the coffin, and deft fingers went rapidly through the dead girl's hair and shroud, and all the pins that could be found on the remains were removed. Then a needle and thread were procured, and the shroud and hair sewn back into their places. The lid was then screwed back on the coffin, and the remains were again lowered into the grave, which was at once filled up.

It was learned that the women were of a very superstitious nature, and that they believed that if a corpse is buried with the shroud pinned up, instead of sewed, the soul will be confined to the grave for eternity, and the persons guilty of the mistake will be haunted till death by the ghost of the victim.

A mistake was made in this case, and one of the women claims that she had seen the ghost for two or three nights successively, and she could stand it no longer; so she got the other women together, and between them they hired the men to disinter the body. The ghost has not been seen since.

The Manchester Evening News, March 10, 1886

Extraordinary Superstition.
Burning Jews' Bones for Typhus

In Galicia a trial has just taken place which reveals extraordinary ignorance and gross superstition among the peasantry of that province. It was discovered at Rzeszow some time ago, says a Vienna correspondent, that several Jewish graves had been broken open, and that the bodies of two children were missing.

The police made inquiries, and found out that in a neighbouring village, where typhus fever had broken out, a so-called 'miracle doctor' had prescribed, as a cure, the burning of the bones of a Jew in the patient's room. When the house of this man was searched, human flesh and bones and a child's skull were found.

The patient had died, notwithstanding the burning of the bones, and the widow of the deceased described how the 'miracle doctor' had set about his cure. He had told her that there were two kinds of typhus. One, the Catholic typhus, could be cured by prayer and exhortation; the other, the Jewish typhus, could only be got rid of by the means described.

He brought the bones himself, with water from a well from which no man had ever drunk, and burnt the bones on a charcoal fire, nearly smothering them all with the terrible fumes.

Then while the room was full of smoke he mumbled some strange words, and hunted round the table, pretending to catch the typhus, which he then put into the water-bottle, and made all present partake of its contents. The 'doctor' was sentenced to five months' imprisonment.

The Citizen, Gloucester, July 26, 1890

Singular Superstition

Dalziel's Agency, dating from Sarnia (Ontario), Nov. 11, states: The members of a religious sect known as 'Israelites' are preparing to migrate to England, being possessed with the idea that the world will shortly come to an end, and that England is the proper place to be in when that event happens.

The York Herald, November 14, 1891

Strange Superstition

An extraordinary case of superstition is reported from Sherborne, in Dorsetshire. In Cold Harbour, on Friday last, an old woman, named Sarah Smith, aged eighty-three, was violently attacked by a next-door neighbour, in order that the latter might 'draw blood,' on the ground that she had bewitched her neighbour's daughter, a confirmed invalid.

The old woman, who is well known as a quiet, inoffensive person, was in her garden when she was attacked, and the blood was 'drawn' by a darning-needle being driven several times into her hands and arms.

The Liverpool Echo, September 30, 1884

Shocking Superstition

An Irish paper reports a case of gross superstition disclosed at a trial at the recent Loughgall (County Antrim) Petty Sessions.

A man named Hagan was summoned by his wife, Sarah Hagan, for gross ill-treatment, the cause of which was the loss of a talisman which Hagan believed enabled him to become invisible at certain times and places.

This mysterious power is communicated by the possession of 'a dead man's finger.' It certainly must have once been part of a very bad man, for its possessor seems to have used it for very bad purposes, his wife having sworn that he kept it because by means of it he could enter any man's dwelling, go behind his counter, and rob his drawers without being observed or detected. This was her evidence, but she could not say if the finger had ever been so employed.

No doubt to a thief such a relic would be valuable. Hagan regarded it in that light; it endowed him with a charmed existence, and, because his wife could not account for it, he gave her a most unmerciful beating, and threatened to take her life. The truth appears to be that the poor woman became alarmed at the conduct of her husband in carrying about the finger, and she buried it in a neighbour's field and forgot the place of interment.

No excuse could satisfy Hagan. He should have the finger and nothing but the finger; so that the poor woman, failing to discover it, felt the power of his fingers in a very unmanly way. The Bench ordered him to find bail to keep the peace for 12 months.

The Taunton Courier, September 23, 1863

A Wonderful Story.
Extraordinary Proceedings

A Shrewsbury correspondent has sent to the *Standard* reports of extraordinary occurrences which took place last week at the village of Weston Fullenfield. A servant named Emma Davies, living with Mr Hampson, a farmer, was discharged, that gentleman and his wife feeling anything but comfortable at her presence.

On Thursday week the girl went to assist Mrs Jones, a neighbour, to wash the household linen, but had not long been engaged in this occupation when the bucket in which she was washing jumped about the house, throwing water and clothes in all directions.

The family Bible and other books placed on a side table did the same, narrowly escaping the flames. On attempting to pick them up a boot flew over the girl's head, striking the mantelpiece.

Later on, when both women went out to place the clothes on the hedge for drying, those that the girl placed jumped over into the road. Mrs Jones, getting alarmed, ordered the girl home.

On arriving there, her presence induced a lump of coal to leap from the fire across the room to a table; and the flowerpots in the window also behaved in an extraordinary manner.

The girl shortly afterwards went out to fetch her father, but before proceeding far she became very ill and fell down in the road. She was conveyed back to her home and a physician called in.

On Saturday afternoon, the correspondent visited the village, and, he says, found sufficient evidence to confirm every detail of the remarkable event. The girl, who is in her thirteenth year, resides in the village with her parents.

On returning to her home on Friday evening, the household and other articles commenced moving about in all directions in the most mysterious manner. This continued during the night. Six panes of glass were broken in the room, and outside the greatest disorder prevailed, and on the side of the house were strewn broken bricks, crockery, glass, stones, &c., which could not be accounted for in any way.

One woman was struck with a stone 150 yards off; another, who was in the house, received a wound on the arm from a knife passing her; and an Ulster belonging to the girl had every button torn from it in the room.

A number of the Shropshire constabulary visited the premises on Saturday to investigate the extraordinary circumstances, but were unable to solve the mystery. The girl was made to do some household work, but nothing unusual was observable. Dr Corke, of Baschurch, was called in on Saturday and made a close examination of the girl, but was unable to obtain much information from her.

He stated that she was in a very excitable and nervous state, but was not a designing girl. The matter is causing the greatest excitement throughout the whole neighbourhood; much superstition prevails in the village.

The Sunderland Daily Echo and Shipping Gazette,
November 13, 1883

Mother Shipton's Prophecies

A very singular cause of death was revealed at an inquest held on the body of a child of 10 years, named Kate Weedon, who resided with her parents at Hoxton.

It appeared that the girl had read the well-known prophecies of Mother Shipton, and had consequently become very much alarmed, the more especially as the present year was quickly drawing to a close. She very frequently cried and talked about the world coming to an end in 1881.

On returning from school on the 17th inst., she was weeping bitterly and speaking of Mother Shipton. Her mother told her it was all nonsense, but this had not the least effect upon her, and when she went to bed at half-past 10 she was still crying and wringing her hands, saying she knew the end of the world would come in the night.

At about half-past 3 on the following morning the mother was awakened by hearing her cry, and on going to her bedroom found the child in a fit.

A doctor was immediately sent for, but his services were of no avail, and the child died two hours later. Medical evidence was to the effect that death was due to convulsions and shock to the system, brought on by fright. A verdict was returned accordingly.

The Taunton Courier, November 30, 1881

~ *Preface* ~

You'd think it far-fetched if it happened in a farce. On a winter's evening in 1874, two burglars crept in to a doctor's surgery in search of loot. While one searched the darkened office with his lantern, his accomplice opened a cupboard, felt blindly inside and promptly got his hand trapped in something painful.

Cue kerfuffle. The man with the lamp swung round, throwing light on an unusual predicament: the thief's fingers were caught in the coil-sprung jaw of a skeleton. Spooked by the sight, he tumbled backwards, pulling the bones upon him and generating enough clatter to rouse the doctor.

This preposterous scene played out first in Greensburg, Pennsylvania, and then shortly afterwards across the pages of a tickled British press, which used crime stories as a kind of journalistic grouting.

Take the *York Herald*, one of the papers to carry the wired report of the hapless exploits of the Greensburg Two. The eight pages of that day's edition brought news of a man kicked to death by drunks; a master mariner who murdered his wife; a violent mugging; a random assault on a passenger at a railway station; a cunning break-in; the theft of weapons from a barracks; and the killing of an insurance agent.

An easily-alarmed reader of the *Herald* might fold the paper and think about bolting the door on the world outside. Yet none of these crimes happened in York itself or the surrounding towns. All the neighbourhood ne'er-do-wells had to offer in response was a pinched umbrella, some nicked boots and a couple of smashed windows.

Like the sworn testimony of an incorrigible liar, Victorian crime statistics should be treated with a certain amount of caution, but it's generally agreed that rates of theft and violence slumped through the second half of the nineteenth century. Yet reality isn't necessarily the same as perception. And for that, newspapers must shoulder a good deal of the blame.

An example. On a July night in 1862, Hugh Pilkington, the MP for Blackburn, was leaving Parliament when he was set upon by two men who knocked him to the ground, choked him and pinched his watch. So began the great garrotting panic of 1862.

Garrotting was a Victorian brand of mugging, with the stylistic tweak of partial strangulation. Even though the actual number of assaults was negligible, the press and public were soon seeing these dastardly types wherever they looked. There's a story of a man walking home in the fog who feared he was being followed by a garrotter, and decided the best form of defence was attack. The innocent chap behind, who'd been merely walking the same way, told the police he'd been garrotted.

Londoners were frightened out of their wits, reported the *Gloucestershire Chronicle* later that year. 'They are afraid to walk the streets after dark and the journals which are supposed to lead public opinion follow it by blowing the flame of general fear.'

The *Chronicle* pointed out the garrotting scare was proving a useful alibi for the louche. 'Does a gent appear at the counting-house in the morning with a terrible headache and a pair of black eyes? He has not been drunk overnight but has been garrotted. Does anybody stay out all night and return in a state of bodily or mental dilapidation? He has not been astray, but has been lying insensible at a hospital, the victim of another outrage of those garrotters. The result of all this is that a large number of amiable and Christian people have come to the conclusion that there really ought to be a good deal more hanging.'

Two years on, a new title hit the newspaper stands: the sensation-hungry *Illustrated Police News*. This journalistic equivalent of a penny dreadful arrived too late for the garrotting panic, but was in pole position for the defining crimes of this or any other age, and it exploited the opportunity ruthlessly. By common consent Jack the Ripper killed five times. *The Illustrated Police News* put him on the front page 184 times.

In between, it titillated and terrified the public with macabre sketches, lurid headlines and a weekly diet of murder and misery served up with unabashed enthusiasm.

If that *York Herald* reader felt a twinge of unease, the average subscriber to the *Illustrated Police News* must have toyed with the idea of stocking up on tinned goods and retiring to a safe room with a blunderbuss and a box of ammunition.

Snake Charmer and Bearded Lady.
A Row in a Show

At Shrewsbury Police Court on Thursday a case of assault which arose between two of the performers at Wombwell's Menagerie was heard.

The complainant was Nina Behnke, or 'Madame Polonoski, the Bearded Lady,' and the defendant Mary Edwards, the snake charmer. There was a visit to the town of Wombwell's Menagerie of wild beasts and other curiosities.

Among the latter was the complainant, who was gifted by nature with a beard. The defendant was a snake charmer. The two ladies were on the stage on Monday night, and in leaving it the complainant accidentally brushed against the dress of the defendant, who thereupon struck the complainant in the face with the head of one of the snakes which she had about her.

Subsequently the defendant, who had hold of a frying-pan, went up to the complainant and assaulted her, knocking her down, giving her two black eyes, and cutting her face and mouth.

The defendant said she was not a pugilist, but a snake charmer. When on the platform she had a chain in one hand, a snake in the other, and two other snakes around her neck. The complainant pushed her and struck her, and also caught hold of one of the snakes, which caused the animal to coil itself tightly around her neck.

The Bench dismissed the case, and ordered each of the ladies to pay her own costs.

The Midland Daily Telegraph, Coventry,
March 12, 1892

Extraordinary Affair

One of the most extraordinary and revolting circumstances has just come to light at a place called Pheasant Hill, two miles from Castlebar.

It seems that a pensioner named Egar and his wife resided for some years past in a lonesome part of the above locality, and the fact of the husband not having made his appearance out of doors for a few weeks caused several inquiries to be made as to his whereabouts.

To each inquiry the wife replied that he was ill and confined to bed, so that he could not be seen.

On Saturday evening, however, one of the neighbours suspecting that all was not right, went to the house, and was told as usual by the wife that her husband was asleep and could not be disturbed. The man, however, insisted on seeing him asleep or awake.

Observing the perseverance and the determination of this man to see her husband, the wife confessed that her husband was dead, and, on going to his room, a frightful spectacle presented itself.

Lying on the floor, covered with mud and 'scraws' was the body of the man, in such a state of decomposition as to make it appear he had been dead for at least three weeks.

The police were at once communicated with, and have now charge of the body pending a coroner's inquiry. The reason assigned for this strange conduct on the part of the woman is, that the quarter's pension of her husband would come due on Monday, and by concealing the death of her husband she might succeed in defrauding the authorities by receiving the amount of his pension.

The Wrexham Advertiser, July 16, 1864

Remarkable Story

A remarkable instance of a dream coming true is reported from St Louis. A woman named Mary Thornton has been detained in custody for a month, charged with the murder of her husband.

She requested to see one of the judges a week ago, and told him that she had dreamed that a man named George Ray murdered her husband, and at the same time gave the Judge full details of the tragedy as seen in her vision.

Ray was not then suspected, but the judge caused a search to be made for him. The man was found on Thursday and charged with the murder, the details, as the woman had given them, being recited to him. Ray was astonished and confessed. The woman was released.

The Worcestershire Chronicle, August 26, 1899

Extraordinary Scene in a Police Court

The utmost consternation was caused among the prisoners at the Birmingham Police Court, on Wednesday morning, by the sudden appearance of a bear in their midst.

Bruin made his entrance from the cells below, and as he thrust his head above the stairs one of the occupants of the dock made a desperate effort to leap over the front in his fright.

For the moment the whole court was surprised at the unusual visitant, but the astonishment gave place to roars of laughter when Bruin's presence was explained.

It appeared that some zealous constable found the animal

that morning performing under the direction of two Frenchmen, and at once took all three into custody.

The dockkeeper, being ignorant of the remarkable capture, stood dumbfounded as the ungainly brute made its startling entry into the court, and while its owners retreated to the back of the court the animal reared itself above the railings of the dock, exhibiting a formidable front to the magistrates, and causing a general scramble from its vicinity.

The policeman charged the Frenchmen with causing an obstruction in the streets, but the magistrates laughed at the complaint, and discharged the remarkable 'trio' on the men promising to leave the town.

As they left the court the bear was made to descend the staircase on its hind legs amid roars of laughter from the spectators.

The Manchester Courier and Lancashire General Advertiser,
April 29, 1882

A Thief Detected by a Parrot

A thief was detected in a singular manner in Gloucester on Tuesday. Mrs Fisher, flour-dealer, of Northgate Street, while in the parlour adjoining her shop, was startled by a parrot which she keeps in her shop loudly calling 'Shop, Fisher, shop,' and hastened to see what was the matter.

Not perceiving any person there, however, she was about to return again to the parlour, when the parrot again commenced screaming and repeating its former words. Mrs Fisher thereupon conceiving that there must be some cause for the extraordinary cries of the bird, walked round the shop, and on the inside of the counter, close to the till, she discovered a little urchin, about eight years old, crouching down to escape notice.

He had opened the till, and had 4½d in coppers in his hands, which he had stolen from it.

The Cornwall Royal Gazette, June 16, 1848

Burglar Caught by a Skeleton

A burglar in Greensburg, Pennsylvania, was recently caught in a remarkable manner. Breaking into a closed and unoccupied office of a physician of that town, the burglar opened a closet (while his companion with a dark lantern was in another part of the room), and, feeling for clothing at about the height of closet hooks generally, got his hands between the jaws of a skeleton, which being adjusted with a coil spring and kept open with a thread, closed suddenly on the intruding hand by the breaking of the thread.

A sudden thought striking the burglar of his being caught by a skeleton in the doctor's closet, so terrified him that he uttered a faint shriek, and when his companion turned the lantern toward him and he beheld himself in the grim and ghastly jaws of Death himself, he became so overpowered by fear that he fainted, fell insensible to the floor, pulling the skeleton down upon him, and making so much noise that his companion fled immediately, and the doctor, alarmed at the noise and confusion, hastened into the office and secured the terror-stricken burglar still held by the skeleton.

The Dundee Courier and Argus, February 26, 1874

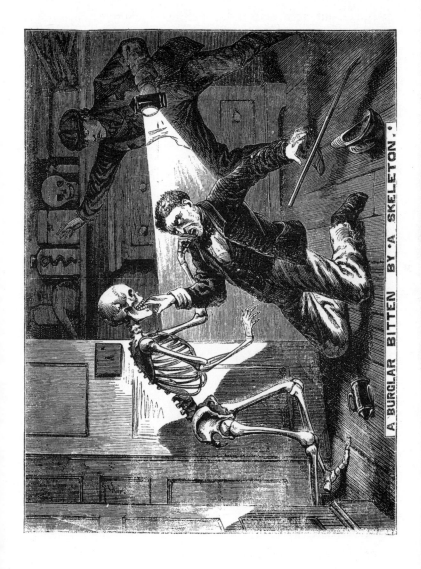

'A BURGLAR BITTEN BY A SKELETON.'

An Elephant in the Witness-Box

A young elephant was introduced into the Court of Exchequer, London, on Friday week, as a witness in an action for damages against Messrs. Bertram and Roberts.

The plaintiff, Miss Thurman, was standing up in an open carriage at the Alexandra Palace when the appearance of this elephant frightened the horse, and the plaintiff, being thrown out, had her collar-bone broken.

Counsel declined to put any question to this novel witness, which, meanwhile, amused itself by seizing the hats upon the table with its trunk. Ultimately the case was arranged.

The Grantham Journal, July 26, 1879

Villa Half-Back Charged with Drunkenness.
The Case Dismissed

Before the Aston Magistrates on Monday, James Cowan, the well-known Aston Villa centre half-back was charged with being drunk on his own premises, the Grand Turk, New Street.

Cowan called a number of witnesses, who declared that so far from being drunk he was able to take a leading part in all intellectual discussion on the Transvaal crisis, the Dreyfus case, and the beauties of Dutch scenery. The proceedings, which lasted two hours, ended in the summons being dismissed.

The Citizen, Gloucester, September 26, 1899

Murderer's Ghastly Mistake.
His Son Changes Beds with his Enemy

An extraordinary story is reported from Tarnopol, in Galicia. A peasant named Adam Gawrydo, whose property is in a small village near Zbaraz, in Galicia, cut his own son's throat with a kitchen knife by mistake.

Some weeks ago a Jewish merchant, Solomon Barb, bought old Gawrydo's stock of honey, and paid 50 florins in advance, to make the bargain valid.

When the time for delivering the honey came, the peasant declared that he could not keep his word, and was prepared to pay any damages to the merchant that the Rabbi might decide.

Yesterday they both went to the Rabbi, who said the peasant must pay the merchant ten florins damages. This he did most willingly, and then both went away together.

On the way home they stopped at a wayside inn, and did not leave it till night. It began to rain, and the peasant asked the merchant to pass the night in his house. The merchant accepted, and they went home together.

The peasant prepared a bed of straw in the barn, and when the merchant had laid down went to his own room after carefully locking the barn door.

This frightened the merchant so much that he got up, felt his way about until he found a second door, which was bolted from the inside, left the barn, and started to walk back to the inn.

In the meantime the son of the peasant returned home half drunk and finding the barn door open walked in and dropped on to the bed of straw prepared for the stranger. He was soon fast asleep. The merchant on his way to the inn met a gendarme, who asked him where he was going so late. Barb told him all that had happened, and the gendarme, thinking he had a dangerous man before him who was lying to avoid suspicion asked him to go with him to the peasant's house.

There they found Gawrydo in the act of washing his hands, which were stained with blood. When he saw them he exclaimed, 'Surely I killed you an instant ago.'

The gendarme searched the house, and in the barn found the son of the peasant dead with his throat cut. The peasant was immediately arrested.

The North-Eastern Daily Gazette, Middlesbrough, July 12, 1894

Extraordinary Case of Attempted Suicide

On Saturday last Mr Sly, landlord of the William the Fourth, Flagon Row, Deptford, discovered that he had been robbed of certain monies, &c., and mentioned the facts to his family and servants. Amongst the latter is a young woman, named Mary Ann Wiggins, who, on hearing the circumstances, became greatly excited and went away.

Shortly afterwards a customer to the house went to the water-closet and found the door fastened within. After waiting a short time the door was forced open, and a noise was distinctly heard of some person struggling in the night soil. On examining the spot the poor creature was discovered immersed over head, scarcely a vestige of her person or dress being discernible.

Less than half a minute's delay and suffocation would have been complete. Assistance was immediately afforded, and with much difficulty she was drawn out of her awful predicament by means of an iron rake which was placed under her arm-pits. This, however, was not effected without bruising and lacerating her person. Mr Downie, who saved the woman's life, says her head was completely under the soil, and it appeared that when he had drawn her partly out she struggled hard to effect her purpose.

Mr Downing, police surgeon, who attended her, states that it was with much time and difficulty that suspended animation could be restored, and that her person was much bruised in getting through the seat of the closet. The place where she was discovered is at least ten feet deep.

On getting out she was stripped by two women in the back yard, and with a large tub of hot water and abundance of soft soap and brushes she was ultimately brought round. Her mouth, nose, and eyes were filled with the night soil, and but for the means so promptly afforded by the surgeon and others her life must have been sacrificed.

After bathing her for a couple of hours by the kitchen fire she was removed to the infirmary of the Greenwich union until convalescent, when she will be taken before the sitting magistrate.

The Northern Star and National Trades' Journal,
London, May 10, 1845

A Naked and Unwelcome Guest

When Charles Warren and his wife, who live at Stepney, got home on Tuesday morning from a party they were surprised to find a naked young man curled up asleep in a perambulator.

The kitchen was in great disorder, and when awakened and asked how he got in, the unwelcome guest replied 'Through the door.'

He was summoned to appear at the Thames Police Court, and a constable said he found one of the windows of the prosecutor's house unfastened. The prisoner's hat was found in one place and his trousers in another. His coat could not be found.

The prisoner, who appeared in a dazed condition, gave a correct address, which was a short distance from the prosecutor's house. The magistrate said there was no evidence that the prisoner intended to steal, and he therefore would be discharged, but he had better be careful for the future.

The Citizen, Gloucester, December 28, 1892

Bound in his Own Skin

Through the courtesy of the librarian of Trinity College, Cambridge, I was enabled (says a correspondent) to examine a portion of human skin which was taken from the body of Corder, the murderer of Maria Martin, in the Red Barn, near Bury St Edmunds.

The doctor who dissected the man after the sentence of death had been carried out, knowing that a 'Life of Corder' was about to be written, sent the author a piece of the murderer's skin, properly tanned and prepared.

In this a copy of the book was subsequently bound and presented to the library. This is a remarkable instance of a man's biography being bound in his own skin.

Supplement to the Hampshire Telegraph and Sussex Chronicle,
December 9, 1893

Singular Trial at Madrid

A most singular trial has taken place at Madrid. A soldier was cited last week before the police court for having stolen a gold cup of considerable value which had been placed as a votive offering on one of the numerous altars dedicated in that city to the Virgin.

The soldier at once explained that he and his family being in great distress he had appealed to the Holy Mother for assistance, and that while engaged in prayer and contemplation of the four millions' worth of jewels displayed on her brocaded petticoat, she stooped, and with a charming smile, handed him the golden cup.

This explanation was received by the court in profound silence, and the case handed over to the ecclesiastical commission, to whom it at once occurred that, however inconvenient the admission of the miracle might be, it would be highly impolitic to dispute its possibility.

They therefore gave the cup to the soldier, at the same time solemnly warning him for the future against similar favours from images of any kind, and impressing him with the conviction that the Virgin required profound silence from him as a proof of his gratitude.

Supplement to the Nottinghamshire Guardian, September 9, 1864

A Chelsea Girl Breaks the Record

A fat and blushing girl from Chelsea has broken the record at Marlborough Street. Her complaint was rum and coffee, and her actions showed how fearfully strong that Chelsea coffee is.

When the Clerk of the Court yesterday asked the honour of an introduction, she said her name was 'the same as it was before': but he could not remember it, and it had slipped from everybody's memory and it continues in a state of slip.

It ought to be preserved, however, because the recording angel of the law had all these memoranda against her:

1. She got drunk.
2. She got ever so much drunker.
3. She got fired out of a restaurant near the Haymarket.
4. She reached for the constable's eye with her shoe, which she had in her hand, and the constable's eye is all wrong.
5. She threw herself on the pavement and had to be taken in with the official van.
6. She hit the constable again, and knocked his helmet an illegal distance.
7. She rolled all over the street and part of her clothes came off.

8. In riding to the station, she yelled, and she yelled, and she yelled.

9. She drew pictures on the walls of her cell with a button-hook.

10. They were bad pictures, and the damage to the walls is 2s 6d.

This was a large order for the book-keepers of justice to figure out, but they made the whole bill £1 2s 6d.

The Dundee Courier and Argus, September 20, 1889

The Falmouth Riot

Seven soldiers of the Royal Artillery stationed at Pendennis Castle were charged at the Falmouth Police Court yesterday with assaulting the police while in the execution of their duty. From the evidence of the Superintendent and other police officers it appeared that Chudleigh, one of the soldiers, was taken into custody for fighting, and that his six comrades, after procuring swords from the barracks, proceeded to the police station, and by means of threats, obtained Chudleigh's liberation. They afterwards paraded the streets, flourishing their swords, and behaving otherwise in a riotous manner. At the conclusion of the evidence, five of the prisoners – viz., Beaney, Callahan, Connor, McInverney, and Seaham – were sent to prison for six months. Chudleigh was committed for three months, and Barker, who did not get possession of his sword, for one month.

The Sheffield Daily Telegraph, January 17, 1879

The Romance of Crime

A strange story comes from Constantinople. A few nights ago – so runs the version of the affair given in a German paper – three robbers, armed to the teeth, broke into the house of a Prussian living in Constantinople.

Threatening to forthwith murder him if he resisted they compelled the owner to submit to being bound, and then demanded from him his valuables and money. The Prussian at once gave up his gold watch and some £4 of Turkish money which he had in his pockets; but this small booty did not satisfy the robbers.

Again they threatened death, and finally obliged the bound and helpless man to tell them where they could find the key of his business safe. This safe happened to be in a room on the third floor, at the top of the house, and thither the three robbers, having obtained possession of the key, hastened, leaving the owner bound, and threatening to return and shoot him if he called for assistance.

But as they went up stairs, his wife, who had been watching what was taking place from another room, slipped quietly in and cut the bonds of her husband. Arming themselves with revolvers, the pair crept quietly up the stairs, came upon the robbers absorbed in dividing among themselves the contents of the safe, and without a word shot down two of them.

The other threw down his weapons and begged for mercy. Turning the tables upon him, the Prussian bound his late assailant fast, and leaving his wife to watch over him with a loaded revolver in her hand, hastened to the nearest zaptieh station.

There he found the officer in charge absent, and on enquiring for a sub-officer was told that both of the latter were also away. Thereupon the Prussian asked four of the men to accompany him to his house and take the bound burglar into custody.

Arrived in the room where the two men had been shot the zaptiehs looked at the two corpses, looked at the prisoner and recognised in the former the two sub-officers and in the latter the officer of their own guard.

The Ipswich Journal, and Suffolk, Norfolk, Essex and
Cambridgeshire Advertiser, May 4, 1880

A 'Glass Eye' Impostor

At Westminster Police Court, on Friday, a middle-aged, shabbily-dressed man, known by a number of names, including those of McKenzie and Paybourne, in which he has been recently charged, was placed in the dock, on remand, before Mr Sheil, charged with obtaining charitable contributions by fraud.

The prisoner, who has called himself a pianoforte maker, has lost the sight of his right eye. According to the evidence of Coltman, Chief Constable of the Mendicity Society, the prisoner turned his infirmity to account by going to noblemen and charitable people all over the country, to whom he made appeals for assistance to obtain a new glass eye.

He usually represented that he had broken one he had obtained from a charitable institution, though at the time he had four or five glass eyes, which had been procured for him at different times, in his waistcoat pocket.

On the 11th inst. he called on Lord St Oswald, at 11, Grosvenor Place, but his lordship at once recognised him, having heard the glass eye story before when the prisoner called on him at his country seat in Yorkshire, and got a sovereign from him.

Lord St Oswald gave him into custody, after listening to his tale. Mr Sheil sentenced him to three months' hard labour, and said the next imposition would mean 12 months.

Berrow's Worcester Journal, July 25, 1896

Desperate Attack on a Hull Policeman.
Strange Case of Somnambulism.

At the Hull Police Court on Monday, Herman Laman, a German, who appeared in the dock with his head in bandages and his clothes bespattered with blood, was brought before Mr Travis, stipendiary magistrate, charged with being a suspected person, and also with assaulting Police Constable Wright.

From the officer's statement it appeared that the prisoner is a native of a small village in Westphalia, and arrived at Hull on Sunday afternoon, in company with other emigrants, *en route* for New York. At eleven o'clock the same night, Amos Moss, emigrant agent and boarding-house keeper, residing in Grimsby Lane, Hull, reported to the police that Laman was missing, and he requested assistance in seeking him, as he could not speak a word of English, and giving an amount of money in his possession, he (Moss) felt anxious concerning him.

A search was instituted and subsequently Police Constable Wright discovered him sitting on the roof of a house in Barker's

Entry, off Grimsby Lane. It was raining very hard at the time, and he (witness) called to him, but received no answer. With the assistance of Police Constable Porter, Wright obtained a ladder, and ascending to the roof, he requested the prisoner to come down. Instead of answering him the man shot at him with a revolver, but fortunately missed him.

The officer repeated his request, and the prisoner shot at him again. This time the bullet struck Wright on the metal part of his belt, and glanced off harmless. Finding that further parley was useless, witness hurled a brick that happened to be lying with others on the roof and hit him on the head, inflicting a serious wound.

He then got upon the roof, and advanced to the prisoner, who shot at him a third time. Witness gave him more bricks (laughter) and part of a chimney pot (renewed laughter), and after Laman had fired five shots, none of which hit him, he managed to knock the weapon out of his hand.

Determined not to be conquered, prisoner also had recourse to the bricks, and a 'pitched battle' was fought with bricks and tiles on the roof at two o'clock in the morning. Ultimately the German, finding he was getting the worst of it, tore up some tiles and let himself through the roof of a house occupied by a Mr Beecroft, and concealed himself between the ceiling and the roof.

Other policemen having arrived on the scene, the party got into the house, and after making a large hole through the ceiling they succeeded in capturing the prisoner, who was weak with loss of blood from the wounds on his head.

He was secured by ropes, lowered from a window, and conveyed to the police-station in a handcart. Dr Kitching's assistant dressed six severe wounds on the man's head at the station house. Wright was but little hurt.

The prisoner, who is a powerful-looking fellow, stated through Dr Jacobsen, the interpreter, that he was about to emigrate, and it was usual for emigrants to carry revolvers.

He was a somnambulist, and did not know how he got on the roof. When the officer came up to him he thought that robbers were after the money he had about him, and he fired his revolver. Mr Travis expressed his doubt as to the prisoner's sanity, and remanded him.

The Leicester Chronicle and Leicestershire Mercury,
September 8, 1877

Parisine

Ordinary items of local news appear in the French papers under the special rubric of 'Faits Divers.' Many of these *faits divers* are simple canards, but a gem is to be found among them now and then. Take the following, for instance:

'Yesterday a rather funny adventure caused a considerable crowd to collect in front of the Louvre. A butterman from Isigny, after having settled his business at the Halles, took a stroll through the city with a Parisian friend who had undertaken to show him the sights.

'All went well till a bizarre incident occurred to trouble the harmony existing between the two friends. Each of them had with him a black wolf-dog, and the two animals, I mean the quadrupeds, were so exactly alike, that their owners on separating could not agree on the identity of their respective property. An altercation ensued and the police had to interfere.

'The disputants were taken before the police commissary. That worthy magistrate, somewhat perplexed by the event, ordered both dogs to be strangled for having been allowed to go about the street without a muzzle. This contemporary judgment of Solomon was applauded by the crowd.'

The Manchester Evening News, May 13, 1884

The Clifton Bridge Sensation

In the presence of a crowded court, the trial took place before Justice Wills, at the Bristol Assizes, on Tuesday, of Charles Albert Browne (36), grocer, Longmore Street, Birmingham, for attempting to drown his two children, Ruby (12) and Elsie (3), by throwing them from Clifton Suspension Bridge into the river Avon in the early hours of the morning of September 18th.

Public interest was specially manifested in the case from the fact that only once previously has anyone gone over the bridge into the water, a distance of over 250 feet, without being killed instantly, and the escape of the little girls is probably attributable to the same cause as in that instance – a strong wind inflating their clothes and regulating their descent.

Some time before the judge arrived a large crowd assembled in front of the Guildhall, and when his Lordship took his seat in court all the available room was occupied, a large proportion of the spectators being ladies.

The elder of the two girls was in the caretaker's room in the building in charge of her mother and a nurse from the Infirmary. During the Assizes she had been observed in the corridors of the court or in the privileged gallery above the bench, and apparently she has recovered from the shock sustained. Mr Douglas Metcalfe conducted the prosecution, and the defence was entrusted to Messrs. Fred E. Weatherly and Thornton Lawes.

The prisoner appeared quite self-possessed, and sat with his hands lightly clasped together during the counsel's opening. He apparently listened with interest to the story of the events in which he was a prominent figure, and occasionally he raised his eyes to the bench or gallery, and scanned the faces of the spectators.

After the evidence, the jury consulted for a few minutes, and then, in answer to the Clerk of Assize, said they found the prisoner guilty of the charge against him, but he was insane at the time, and not responsible for his actions.

The judge thereupon ordered him to be detained in the prison till her Majesty's pleasure was known.

The Tamworth Herald, December 5, 1896

Curious Law Case in France

A very curious case has just come before the juge de paix of Neuilly. Some time ago, Madame Pluyette, a widow lady of 50, but who still attaches much importance to personal appearance, had the misfortune, in playing with a lap-dog, to receive from it so severe a wound in one of her eyes that it came out of the socket.

Having heard much of artificial eyes, and being recommended to apply to an expert manufacturer in this way, named Tamisier, she gave an order for a glass eye, for which M. Tamisier charged her 100 francs.

Refusing to pay this charge, the manufacturer summoned her before the juge de paix. Madame Pluyette having appeared holding the glass eye in her hand, the juge de paix asked her why she refused to pay the bill which M. Tamisier had sent in?

'For a very good reason,' replied the defendant. 'I can see no more with it than I could before.'

'What!' said the juge de paix, 'did you really imagine that you would be able to see with a glass eye?' 'Did I think so?' retorted the angry dame, 'certainly I did. Will you be so good as to tell me what eyes are for, but to see with? I ordered the eye for use, and, until M. Tamisier makes me one with which I can see, I will not pay him a sou.

'I wear a wig, which is quite as useful as natural hair. I have three false teeth, which answer as well as those which I have lost, and why should I pay for an eye which is of no use?'

The juge de paix endeavoured to convince Madame Pluyette that glass eyes were for others to look at, and not for the wearers to look from them; but, finding all appeals to her reason of no avail, he condemned her to pay the plaintiff the amount of his demand.

When the defendant heard the decision, she became furious with anger, and, after dashing her glass eye on the floor, she rushed out of court amid the laughter of the crowd.

The Leicester Journal, October 9, 1846

A Murderer Hunted Down by a Woman

A remarkable arrest has been effected at Oklahoma by a girl. In November last two men named James Heath and Walter Hargood quarrelled over a young woman, and in the course of the dispute, Hargood shot his rival.

Heath's sister, intent on bringing her brother's murderer to justice, donned male attire, and otherwise disguised herself, and after much hardship, succeeded in tracking Hargood to this vicinity, where she gave information to the police. Hargood was at once arrested.

The Yorkshire Evening Post, April 25, 1892

A Wife Beater

An inhabitant of a village near Coleford recently beat his wife and threatened mischief to his child. A neighbour, overhearing the strife, rushed in and took from him a knife with which he vowed he would wreak further vengeance.

Another person started for the police, but protection was nearer at hand. The news having spread, about forty women waited on the wife-beater. As soon as he saw this display of 'reserve forces' he bolted upstairs, but was soon compelled to come down.

Then, in a manner unmentionable to ears polite, these Amazonian women administered the punishment so familiar to English boys, and in no respect less severe or mortifying in its character.

They next carried their victim to the millpond hard by, with the intention of immersing him. He begged hard for mercy, and was at length let off with a few buckets of water thrown over him. After this he solemnly fell on his knees and promised that he would never molest his wife again, and was then allowed to depart 'a sadder and wiser man.'

The Citizen, Gloucester, August 16, 1878

✑ WAGERS ✑

On July 17, 1856, a terrible train crash claimed the lives of 60 passengers in Pennsylvania. In Madrid the same day, a bloody battle between the National Guard and Royal troops left bodies strewn in the streets. And in St James's Street, London, Mr F. Cavendish bet Mr H. Brownrigg that he wouldn't kill the fly that was bothering him before he went to bed.

The bluebottle met its match. We know that thanks to the scuffed-up, defaced old betting book at White's gentlemen's club. 'Recd, HB', it says, beneath the record of the wager.

When they weren't dining lavishly or dozing flatulently in armchairs, they liked a flutter at White's. Actually, that's an understatement. Once, when a passer-by was brought in having collapsed in the street outside, the assorted aristocrats laid odds on whether he'd live or die. On another occasion, Lord Cobham bet a Mr Nugent that he could spit in Lord Bristol's hat without repercussions. Lord Alvanley, an inveterate gambler who came into a fortune and applied himself to getting rid of it as speedily as possible, reputedly bet on a race between two rain drops down the club's window. The stake? £3,000, roughly 300 times the annual earnings of a general servant.

The terms were dutifully recorded in the book, which

was published in 1892. Some of the wagers are born of the kind of disputes that could be settled in moments today on the internet. Squabbles about the correct wording of a French phrase, for instance, or whether an obscure general was alive or dead. Many of the rest were predictions; on politics, high society or the justice system. Would Lord Derby's government survive the new year? Would the Duchesse de Montpensier have a child before her sister? Would the prince of poisoners William Palmer swing for his crimes? Would Baron de Vidil be sentenced to hard labour for horse-whipping his son? Idle bets, of the idle rich.

But while gambling was rife among the upper classes, society took a dimmer view of the masses joining in. 'There can be no doubt that the vice of gambling is on the increase amongst the English working-classes', tutted James Greenwood in *The Seven Curses of London* in 1869, pointing to the spiralling numbers of sports papers published in the capital as proof.

The government made a couple of spirited attempts to stamp it all out, but to little ultimate effect. And as the decades passed, and Victorians refined the art of free time, there were so many new things to bet upon: football matches, cricket tests, rugby games …

Alternatively, you could simply make up your own challenge. In Brixton Deverill, in Wiltshire, in 1883, two farmers had a bet to see who could eat the most hard-boiled eggs. After they had scoffed 28 each, the battle was abandoned. No winner, then, but it's safe to say the village nightsoil man was the loser.

A Foolish Election Wager

Anderson (Indiana), Monday: An unfortunate election enthusiast here will probably die in consequence of a foolish bet. He wagered that if Mr Cleveland carried the State he would swallow a live turtle, and he has honestly done so, the specimen being small but lively. Now it refuses to digest, or even to die, and is causing the man frightful agony besides. The doctors are trying to dislodge or kill it, but without success.

The Western Mail, Cardiff, November 15, 1892

Killed by Cigarettes

As the result of an attempt to see how many cigarettes he could smoke in half an hour to win a wager, a fourteen year old lad named Elwell, of Chicago, has just met with his death.

It appears from the *New York Tribune* that a number of newsboys were talking of cigarette smoking, and one of the crowd urged Elwell to see how many he could smoke in half an hour. A small wager was made, and two packets of cigarettes were purchased. The lad was taken sick during the night and he died in the morning.

The Loughborough Herald and North Leicestershire Gazette,
September 3, 1896

A Peculiar Bet

A Lyons boatman, named Aymard, has just won a considerable sum of money. He bet he would descend the Saone from Thoissey to Lyons on a piece of ice floating down the river.

He embarked at Thoissey last Sunday evening on a sheet of ice four metres long by three metres broad, and took a portable stove and the materials to make pancakes, which was one of the stipulations of the wager.

On Tuesday morning he reached Lyons safely. While passing under the bridges he attached the pancakes he had made to strings which were let down to him by the cheering crowd.

He landed at the appointed spot, and received quite an ovation, while his ice craft continued floating down the river, carrying the tricolour flag he had planted on it.

The Blackburn Standard and Weekly Express, February 28, 1891

Extraordinary Wager by a Boy

On Tuesday a boy named John Magee, aged 16, was admitted to the Cardiff Infirmary under most singular circumstances.

It appears that while playing with other lads Magee undertook, for a small wager, to swallow fifty-three marbles. He succeeded, and apparently suffered no discomfort. His friends, however, became alarmed on hearing of the affair, and escorted him to the infirmary, where he was detained, seemingly none the worse for his extraordinary feat. Yesterday the medical staff succeeded in extracting forty-three of the marbles.

The Western Daily Press, Bristol, November 12, 1891

In the Lions' Cage

A High Wycombe resident has attained to the distinction of a hero by reason of a curious wager into which he entered on the closing night of the town's Michaelmas fair.

He volunteered to enter a cage of forest bred lions which formed part of a travelling circus, smoke a cigar, and drink a bottle of champagne to the health of his Wycombe friends.

The eventful hour arrived, and with the greatest nonchalance, the hero entered the cage and performed his feat, gaining the applause of the townspeople assembled. No one else could be found who would follow his example.

The Yorkshire Telegraph and Star, Sheffield, September 28, 1899

An Amusing Scene in Sheffield

Yesterday a crowd gathered on the canal bank, near Messrs. Turton's bridge, to witness the issue of a singular wager.

A man named Carrol had made a bet that he could pull a cat across the water, and the wager had provided ample food for bar-parlour gossip. Carrol stood on one bank of the canal, and the cat was held on the other. Pussy had a rope round its body, and the other end of the rope was placed round Carrol's waist.

At a given signal, when Carrol began to pull at the cat, some wags on the opposite bank seized the rope and dragged Carrol himself into the water, so that he not only lost the bet, but was the object of much mirth, although the 'carol' to which he gave expression when he got out of the canal had little that was joyous about it.

The Sheffield and Rotherham Independent, August 27, 1883

A Mad Wager

A curious wager with fatal results was recently decided at Siepring, in Bavaria (says *Vanity Fair*). A notoriously strong man, named Freytag, betted that a horse could not move him from the door of his house.

The horse was brought, and Freytag put his hands and feet against the door-posts, whilst Stern, the man with whom the bet was made, fixed a rope round Freytag's neck.

At the first pull the rope broke. A new rope having been brought, Stern plied his whip with all his might, when Freytag gave a scream, and, letting go, was dragged along for some yards. His neck was broken.

The Citizen, Gloucester, August 25, 1890

An Extraordinary Wager

The eccentric individual who a short time since undertook for a wager of a thousand francs to travel from Romorantin to Paris on foot, escorted by fifty rabbits, and accomplish the distance in the space of five days, encouraged by the successful issue of his first enterprise, has just announced his willingness to start on a second expedition of a similar nature.

The difficulties he encountered on the first occasion were not slight. A fortnight before starting he selected, he says, 25 male and 25 female rabbits, which troop he endeavoured to accustom to the work cut out for them by training them to the required indifference to dogs, carriages, and other objects liable to alarm their timid nature.

At the outset the rabbits proved distressingly refractory. At every noise, every sound, they scampered away right and left, helter-skelter, refusing to be coaxed back into order, causing thus much precious time to be lost.

In despair at the prospect of losing both the wager and his reputation, their leader tried the effect of a stimulant; to each rabbit he administered a small dose of eau-de-vie, which appears to have supplied the troop with a courage foreign to their nature.

No longer timorous, they bounded forward with such speed that their owner had some difficulty in keeping up with them, arriving in Paris some hours before the expiration of the time fixed for the singular excursion.

Proud of his achievement, he has just offered to accept bets with any one disposed to make them for his second enterprise. This time, confident in his rabbits, especially when under the influence of brandy, he proposes to perambulate the Paris Exhibition at midday on any given Sunday, and to make his exit without there being one of the animals lacking.

After the accomplishment of this feat he backs himself, and invites others to back him, for an excursion to Berlin, which city he promises to reach in twenty-two days with his troop of rabbits intact.

The Edinburgh Evening News, June 19, 1878

———◆———

A Suicidal Wager

The prevalent mania for performing insane feats of endurance appears to have 'caught on' in India, with results that might have been anticipated.

With an ardent desire for fame and with stupid originality, a Mahommedan made a wager with a co-religionist that he would stand gazing at the Indian sun for 10 hours on end.

On the appointed day, at eight o'clock in the morning, the aspirant to immortality took up his position face to face with the sun-god. As the hours went by a vast crowd of excited sportsmen surrounded the man and eagerly looked on while he was suffering visible defeat.

At three o'clock he fell down in a fit, beaten by three hours, and very shortly afterwards he died.

Supplement to the Manchester Courier and
Lancashire General Advertiser, October 23, 1886

———

Death Follows a Wager.
A Story with a Moral

The London *Mail*'s Paris correspondent says that two men in a tavern in the Latin quarter were boasting of their drinking powers, and one wagered twenty francs with the other that he could drink twenty-four absinthes.

He won the bet, and proceeded home. Shortly afterwards his companion, who lived in the same house, left the tavern for his house. As he mounted the staircase he found the drinker dead, hanging over the banisters. He was so horrified that he fell down the stairs and broke his leg.

The Midland Daily Telegraph,
Coventry, February 3, 1899

Extraordinary Brutality

We are informed that on the afternoon of Thursday last, a village not a hundred miles from Kegworth was the scene of a most extraordinary, and, at the same time, most disgusting incident.

A man, it is alleged, made a wager that he would kill a rat by worrying it to death with his mouth. The bet was at once accepted; upon which a live rat was produced and placed upon the table of a public house, and its escape prevented by a cord of the length of three-quarters of a yard being placed round its neck, and fastened to a nail inserted in the wood.

The fellow thereupon commenced his pursuit of the frightened animal, and it was only with considerable difficulty that it was at length secured. The man's object was to seize the rat with his mouth by the back of the neck; and for this purpose he made a series of lunges with his head. One snap, however, having failed, the rat at once buried its teeth in his cheek, making it bleed most profusely.

This unexpected rebuff at once aroused the rage and fury of the assailant, who immediately renewed the attack, and plunged his teeth in the belly of the animal, which still clung to his face.

The consequence was that the rat was compelled to relax its hold; fell upon the table half-dead; was once more attacked by its inhuman foe, bitten on the back of the neck, and speedily thereafter dispatched.

Incredible as it may seem, it is stated that the same fellow, and another equally brutal, have offered to test at no distant date which can thus cruelly massacre the largest number of such vermin in a specified time; but it is earnestly to be hoped that the police will interfere to prevent more of such cruel and ferocious so-called 'sport.'

The Leicester Chronicle and Leicestershire Mercury,
February 26, 1876

A Fatal Wager

One day last week, says the Spanish paper *Eco del Navarra*, a wager was made between two men, which ended in the death of one of them and the narrow escape of the other.

The object of the bet was to see which of them, after remaining a day without food, should be able to drink 17 glasses of strong wine, and then walk from Pampeluna to Eransus, a place about 6½ miles distant.

As one of them was much younger than the other he agreed to carry a pound of earth for every year by which his competitor was his senior. Since their respective ages were twenty-six and forty-two, the younger man had to carry 16 pounds of earth.

After the fast agreed upon they drank their 17 glasses (about 6¼ English pints each), and set out on the journey. They had not gone far when the elder of the two fell and the younger lay down.

On being carried to a bed in a neighbouring house, the man who had fallen shortly after died; while he with the weight has escaped death only by the skin of his teeth.

Both men were Frenchmen, and the incident shows that, in other countries besides England, mad bets are made.

The Manchester Evening News, June 3, 1879

A Strange Wager

Vienna, Wednesday night. A curious wager is at present occupying the attention of such widely separated classes as our young noblemen and the Association of Hotel and Restaurant Waiters in the capital.

Several of the younger scions of the highest Austrian aristocracy, who were accustomed to dine in an old hotel of high repute in the Karnthner Strasse, took exception to the practice of the waiters, most of whom had seen twenty or thirty years service, in dressing their moustaches in just the same fashion as the 'noble swells' they had to serve.

One of the high-born customers accordingly laid a wager with some of his friends, which was immediately accepted, that within a given time the objectionable adornment should disappear from the upper lips of the waiters in all the fashionable hotels and restaurants in Vienna, otherwise the proposer himself was to shave off his own embellishment for a given period.

In order to effect his purpose, the latter commenced by trying to persuade the hotel keeper in the Karnthner Strasse to forbid all his servants wearing moustaches, on penalty of losing his aristocratic customers.

In this case he succeeded, but the waiters, who were mostly married men, one after another gave notice to leave their places. They were at once replaced by younger men, who, for a consideration, submitted to the imposed humiliation.

The same thing happened in a number of other hotels and restaurants, and the wager was nearly won by the layer when the proprietor of the Hotel Imperial, the first hotel in Vienna, flatly refused to comply with the whim of the Vienna *jeunesse dorée*, whom he told outright that if they deserted his house he should readily find better customers.

The case was also taken up 'as a matter of right and honour,' by the Association of Waiters, which threatened to expel from the Society any member degrading himself by humouring aristocratic caprice in this matter.

Thus the matter stands at the present moment. The bet appears likely to be lost, and then will come the triumph of the waiters, who expect soon to have the satisfaction of seeing their would-be dictator instead of themselves going about with shaven lips.

The Nottingham Evening Post,
October 16, 1890

Peculiar Bets

Peculiar bets on the outcome of the Presidential election are causing considerable amusement in the Western States.

If Mr McKinley is elected, Henry Winsted, of Kinkley Junction, Indiana, is to engage in a butting match with a full grown ram; while should Mr Bryan be the victor, John Burns, of the same town, will drink three pints of hard cider while standing on his head in a barrel.

Arthur Williams, of Burr Oak, Michigan, has agreed to support the mother-in-law of his neighbour, George Stebbens, if the Democrats win, while if they lose Mr Stebbens will twist the tail of a vicious mule owned by Williams once a day for three weeks.

The strangest bet of all has been made by George Wren, of Deepwells, Wisconsin, and Samuel Carpenter, of a neighbouring town. If the former, who is an ardent Bryanite, loses, he is to wear all his clothes backward during the next four years, and if he wins, the other man is to walk backwards during Mr Bryan's incumbency of office, and is to eat crow pie every day for breakfast.

The Star, Guernsey, August 30, 1900

ACCIDENTS and DISASTERS

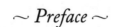

~ *Preface* ~

The memorial is a study in anguish. A grieving mother, carved from marble, tips back her head in distress, the body of a lifeless child draped across her arm. It stands encased in glass in Sunderland's Mowbray Park, just across the road from the scene of one of the most harrowing episodes in the disaster-strewn span of nineteenth-century Britain.

Victorian society never seemed far from catastrophe. In 1878, more than 650 people died on a pleasure trip down the Thames when the SS *Princess Alice* was split in two by the collier *Bywell Castle*. A year later, the storm-lashed Tay Bridge collapsed, taking the train from Wormit to Dundee too. Fishing fleets from the Moray Firth and Eyemouth were lost at sea. Warships and passenger liners sank. A burst dam sent a wall of water cascading through Sheffield. Calamitous military adventures befell in Afghanistan, the Crimea and South Africa. There were explosions and collapses at mines in Lanarkshire, Glamorgan, Northumberland, Yorkshire, Leicestershire and more.

Yet there was nothing quite like the Victoria Hall tragedy, a disaster that claimed almost twice as many lives as at Hillsborough football stadium – all of them children – but has slipped from the collective memory.

The kids had come to see the Fays, a pair of travelling entertainers who promised the 'greatest treat for children ever given': conjuring, talking waxworks, living marionettes and 'the great ghost illusion'.

'Every child entering the room will stand a chance of receiving a handsome present of books, toys etc' said the handbill they'd given out at schools.

The show started at three o'clock that Saturday afternoon in June 1883, and drew to a close two hours later as the Fays performed their finale, during which they threw toys into the pit below the stage.

'This way for the prizes', called a voice, and the boys and girls in the gallery above, fearing they'd miss out, stampeded for the stairs. The staircase led down to a door that opened inwards and was bolted ajar, leaving a gap just big enough for a child to squeeze slowly through.

Within minutes, a crush had built up. A coachman called Fred Bonner, hearing the cries from the hall, dashed in and began pulling children through the gap, then took an axe to the door in desperation. The heavy iron bolt holding it shut was found later to have bent by an inch.

In all, 183 children died that afternoon. Thirty of them came from one Sunday school class, reported the *Sunderland Daily Echo and Shipping Gazette* on the following Monday. 'In one house in the west end, there are four children lying dead. Two of them are laid out upon a little table and the others are laid upon a piano. We also learn that a suffering father was carrying a dead child in each arm from the Victoria Hall when his wife met him, and utterly unnerved, he fell to the ground with his melancholy burden.'

The bodies were laid out in a theatre that had turned into a morgue. 'A man and his wife rushed in,' said the *Echo*, 'the man eagerly scanned the faces of the dead, and without betraying any emotion, said with his finger pointed and with face blanched, "That's one," and passing on two or three yards, still pointing, "That's another;" and still walking on, pointing to the last child in the row, he uttered, "Good God! All my family gone!" and staggering back he cried out "Give me water, give me water."'

Shocking Ice Accident in Regent's Park.
Forty Persons Drowned

About three o'clock on Tuesday, while a large number of persons were skating on the ornamental water in Regent's Park the whole sheet of ice, several hundred yards long and probably two hundred and fifty yards across, first bending in the middle, gave way, and broke into myriads of pieces.

Scarcely any of the 200 or more on the ice escaped immersion. Some managed to float on large isolated pieces of ice to the shore; many were struggling in the water for their lives, and when all seen struggling had been rescued it was generally supposed that a number, variously estimated at from twenty to fifty, were still in the water.

Efforts were at once made by means of the few boats at

hand to drag for the bodies, and one by one they were recovered, though after such terrible delay as rendered resuscitation almost hopeless.

The actual scene of the catastrophe was the Ornament Water, immediately in front of the Essex Place. Upon this, during the whole day, there was a large concourse of skaters assembled, many of whom were attracted thither probably by the fineness and smoothness of the ice.

At four o'clock the number was diminished to a few hundreds, but the sport was spiritedly maintained. The first and only signal of danger was the breaking of the ice as near as possible in the middle, where one boy only was immersed. Almost simultaneously the whole sheet of ice gave way.

In a moment the scene was transformed to one of the most heartrending character. A few minutes sufficed to clear the surface of any visible sign of life. The little island, and the hither shore, were bestrewed with drenched persons, some gratulating themselves on their fortunate escape, others alarmed for the safety of some friend with whom he had just before been sharing his enjoyments.

We may mention one melancholy incident of the disaster. A gentleman living in Euston Square, whose body was recovered by the boatmen, though at first thought to be dead, revived under the treatment he received, and his first exclamation was, 'Where is my son? my only son?' – who, it appears, had been skating with his father, and who it is feared is among the drowned.

Up to six o'clock, half-a-dozen bodies only had been recovered, but the boatmen were still at work by torchlight dragging for the bodies. The scene around was then of a most painful character.

Men and women were there in grief, and anxious after the safety of relatives; scores were still left on the island, unable to get ashore, suffering no little misery in their drenched condition.

The Derbyshire and Chesterfield Herald,
January 19, 1867

Strange Story of a Broken Wooden Leg

At the Gingerbread Fair yesterday (writes the Paris correspondent of the London *Evening News*) a young man named Thinet was imprudent enough to venture too close to a velocipede roundabout, and being caught by the leg in the machinery, was whirled along for several yards head downwards, and picked up in a fainting condition, with a broken leg.

On the way to the chemist's shop near at hand Thinet became completely unconscious, and remained so until the arrival of the surgeon. While the latter was cutting away the rags of trouser from the broken limb Thinet came to, and in spite of the pain in which he presumably was in, began to laugh.

The broken leg was a wooden one, and he had escaped with nothing more severe than a bad headache and a bruise or two.

The queerest part of the adventure was, however, the arrival on the scene of another man who, while peacefully taking a glass of absinthe at a little cafe opposite the merry-go-round, was severely wounded in the face by the other half of the leg which had flown off at a tangent, broken a window, and hit him on the forehead.

The Manchester Evening News, April 12, 1899

———

Extraordinary Accident

A singular accident has occurred at Wolverhampton. A domestic servant, named Hannah Bate, in the employ of Mr Willcock, builder, was in the kitchen of her master's house, when a portion of the flooring immediately over the soft water cistern suddenly gave way, and the girl fell into the well beneath, which contained six feet of water.

Mr Willcock, hearing the girl's screams for help, ran into the kitchen, but, not perceiving what had happened, he too fell into the cistern. Fortunately, a policeman passing by, hearing the calls for assistance, entered the house, and, finding what had happened, set to work to rescue the master and servant.

Whilst so engaged another portion of the covering, on which he was standing, gave way, and he also went down into the water. The services of a second policeman were quickly procured, and he, with assistance, succeeded in drawing the two men and the girl out of the cistern.

The girl is suffering from shock to the system, but Willcock and the policeman are none the worse for the wetting.

The Illustrated Police News, February 13, 1886

———

A Peculiar Accident

Madame Coanda, wife of the military attaché of the Roumanian Legation in Paris is the victim of a peculiar accident. She was on a visit to the Comtesse d'Ormesson, who resides in the Avenue d'Iona. In the house is a lift for the convenience of those residing in the upper flats, but without any attendant specially set apart to work it, the practice being for residents and visitors to put it into motion themselves.

Madame Coanda entered the apparatus and started it, but on reaching the flat occupied by the Comtesse she became flurried and forgot to stop it. The lift continued its ascent. Madame Coanda, who is evidently unacquainted with the working of these useful inventions, become frightened that when it reached the top it would turn over and fall with her to the ground.

In this she was mistaken, as it would have stopped automatically the moment it reached the highest floor. When the lift arrived at the next storey she jumped, in her terror, through the glass door, and fell, fainting and bleeding, on the floor of the corridor.

The Comtesse d'Ormesson sent for a doctor speedily, who found Madame Coanda injured considerably, and cut about the face by pieces of broken glass. She was conveyed afterwards to her own residence in the Rue Marbeuf, and the medical man attending her states that she is recovering satisfactorily.

The Huddersfield Chronicle and West Yorkshire Advertiser,
July 12, 1890

Extraordinary Freak of a Lad

On Tuesday morning some consternation was felt in Plantation Street, Rhymney, by an extraordinary explosion.

It appears that in a house at the lower part of the street were five children, among whom was a lad apparently about 14 or 15 years old. This wicked urchin by some means got possession of a quantity of blasting powder, which he threw, bit by bit, into the fire.

Becoming bolder, and not heeding the warning of a girl, he threw the bag of powder, and all its contents, into the fire. It immediately exploded, causing such a severe shock that the adjoining houses shook to their foundations, and, in some instances, beds were entirely lifted from their places, and their occupants terribly shaken and frightened.

The young delinquent, together with the girl and a baby, have been severely burnt about their heads and faces. The house was scorched, and literally riddled with gunpowder marks.

Two children at the time of the explosion were lying in bed, and had not help been procured immediately – the door having been shut by the young culprit running away – both would, undoubtedly, have been suffocated by the smoke which filled the house.

*Supplement to the Manchester Courier and
Lancashire General Advertiser*, October 10, 1874

Gruesome Curiosity.
Fall Through a Mortuary Skylight

On Thursday evening a peculiar incident occurred at the Hartlepool Mortuary. Two young working men, in their overweening desire to inspect the mangled remains of Mr Riley (whose sad death was recorded yesterday), repaired thither.

Finding the door locked, the more venturesome of the pair climbed on to the roof to peer through the skylight. Whilst so engaged, the glass gave way beneath his weight, and he fell through the aperture on to the top of the dead body, himself receiving rather severe cuts from the broken glass.

The door being locked, the inquisitive intruder could only be liberated on his companion fetching the police.

The Yorkshire Evening Post, August 26, 1893

An Unfortunate Depositor

A peculiar incident in connection with the recent bank failures has occurred at Wigan. A few weeks ago an old man, who had deposited his savings in the Wigan branch of Parr's Banking Company, became alarmed as to the security of his money, and like a large number of persons situated in a similar position in the district, determined to withdraw the amount.

Accordingly, on presenting himself at the Wigan Bank, he received the sum in notes, seven £100 and four £5 notes, total £720. Yesterday the depositor attended at the bank with his notes in a sad mess. On taking home the cash he appears to have placed the notes in a drawer in the house, where they were got at by the mice, and these little animals have had an expensive meal, all of the notes are more or less eaten away.

The notes will be forwarded to the Bank of England, and everything done to enable the man to recover his money.

The Edinburgh Evening News, December 17, 1878

A Dangerous Experiment

Whilst the gallows in Duke Street Prison, Glasgow, which was to be used to-day for the execution of the Port Glasgow murderers, was being tested under the personal direction of Marwood, one of the workmen put his head into the noose. Scarcely had he done so, when either his foot slipped or the trap gave way, and unfortunately the man got a drop that almost hanged him.

The Manchester Evening News, May 23, 1883

Extraordinary Adventure of a Runaway Boy

A boy named Edward Light, ten years of age, has been received into the Bedminster Union Workhouse reduced almost to a skeleton, and who was discovered in the trunk of a tree at Long Ashton.

He tells a most extraordinary and well nigh incredible story. He stated that about a week since he left home because he had spent his school-money, and having been pushed into some water in the People's Park he walked about until the evening, when he pulled his boots off because they were wet, and crept for shelter into the hollow trunk of an elm-tree.

His feet then became benumbed and swollen, so that he could not put on his boots and could not walk, and he was unable to extricate himself from his voluntary prison. All he could do was to put his hand through a hole in the tree to endeavour to attract attention, and it was this signal and his moans which at last brought him aid.

He was rescued by two men named Bryant and Cook, employed by the Bedminster Coal Company, and was taken in a conveyance to the workhouse. The boy asserts that he was in the trunk of the tree from the day he left home until he was discovered – six days – without food. He has not been allowed to take any solid food yet, but is progressing satisfactorily, though he will probably lose some of his toes.

His parents state that the boy had a good home, that there was no reason for his leaving, and they had been searching for him since the day he was missed.

The boy adheres to his statement that he was in the tree on the Ashton Court Estate from Friday, the 18th December, till Christmas Eve, when his cries were heard. The first day he ate some orange-peel which he had in his pocket. Whenever he heard carts passing on the nearest road he shouted, but his cries were not heard.

He got worse and worse, and suffered greatly from thirst. He was able to lie down in the hollow of the tree trunk, but his hands and feet during the hard frost had got so numbed that he could not use them. He felt worse when the frost came, and he cried all night, and could not sleep.

When the hard weather broke he felt a little better, and then his cries were at last heard by the children in the adjoining lane. He has been visited by his parents, but he cannot yet be removed from the Bedminster Workhouse Infirmary.

The Illustrated Police News, January 9, 1886

American Railway Disaster.
A Singular Explanation

A Chicago telegram says: A confession has been made by a boy, throwing light on the cause of the fatal accident which occurred on the Chicago Rock Island and Pacific Railway last Thursday evening, when the Vestibule express ran into a Blue Island suburban train, wrecking two cars, with disastrous results to life and limb.

The boy, who is only twelve years old, admits that he threw from the rear of the wrecked train a signal fuse, which, it seems, was in the nature of a notification to the train following the suburban train that it was behind time.

The result was that the driver of the express increased speed instead of slacking as he would otherwise have done. The boy declares that he did not know what the signal was for, and has been released. Of the seventeen persons injured in the accident seven have since died, bringing up the total loss of life to twelve.

The Evening Telegraph and Star, Sheffield,
November 14, 1893

Fearful Situation of
a Female Somnambulist

On Tuesday last week a scene of a harrowing nature was witnessed by many of the inhabitants of Budingen, in Germany. A young lady, named Dorothea Lessing, the daughter of a wealthy merchant, has, for several months past, been in the habit of walking in her sleep. After perambulating for an hour or so in an unconscious state, she usually returned to her sleeping chamber without experiencing any mishap. Not so, however, on the night in question.

It would appear on this occasion that she opened the window of her bedroom, and afterwards endeavoured to cross a small iron bridge which connects the upper storeys of some warehouses to those on the other side of the street. The bridge, which is constructed of very slender ironwork, had not been used for some time, in consequence of a fracture near its centre.

The supposition is that it vibrated beneath the weight of the sleepwalker; but this is merely conjecture. It is certain, however, from some cause or another, that Dorothea Lessing lost her footing, and must have fallen into the street below had not her wrist been caught in one of the apertures of the ironwork. By this she was suspended. A piercing shriek aroused several of the inhabitants of the town, who were horrified at beholding a beauteous young woman in such imminent peril.

The burgomasters, some of whom chanced to be upon the spot, hastened to secure a ladder, which was not sufficiently long for the purpose. Another was brought by a neighbour, the two were lashed together, and the unconscious young lady – who had fainted from fear and pain – was with difficulty

PERILOUS POSITION OF A SOMNAMBULIST.

released. One of the bones of the right arm is seriously injured. The shock to the system is so severe that great doubts are entertained respecting her ultimate recovery.

The Illustrated Police News, February 19, 1870

Three Thousand Lives Lost in Russia

The following extraordinary statement is from the *Cologne Gazette*: The Russian journals announce an unexampled catastrophe at Taganrog, on the Sea of Azoff.

Allured by the mildness of the temperature, and by the purity of a cloudless sky, about 3,000 inhabitants of Taganrog followed the fishermen upon the ice. In that country fishing is the favourite occupation of all – young and old, rich and poor.

The air was so calm that all advanced, without mistrust, farther and farther upon the ice, in the hope of obtaining a richer booty.

Suddenly a warm wind rose from the east, which insensibly rose higher, whirled masses of snow, and finished by detaching from the shore the ice which adhered to it. In a few instants the vast sheet of ice cracked – rose – broke in several places – and the unhappy people who were upon it saw themselves carried out towards the open sea.

Two hours afterwards not a trace of life was perceived from the shore upon the surface of the wave. On the following day the waves drove ashore a floe of ice, on which were five of these unhappy people; three were dead, and others stupefied by cold

– the two last, a young girl and an old man. The young girl died some hours after.

The old man survived, but from fright he had lost the use of his tongue. He gave in writing a narrative of the events of this frightful night. The number of persons who met death in the waves amounts to 3,000.

The Leicester Chronicle,
March 19, 1859

Horse Killed by Bees

An extraordinary accident which was attended with serious consequences, is reported from the village of Snainton, midway between Pickering and Scarborough.

On Wednesday afternoon three waggon loads of beehives, the property of Messrs Hicks & Hearts, were being conveyed from Sherburn to Givendale Head, and about two miles from Snainton the foremost waggon gave a lurch and one of the hives toppled over.

The bees escaped in thousands, and at once attacked the driver and the horse. The poor brute, maddened by the stinging insects, set off at a swinging gallop, and the unfortunate driver, who had himself to screen from the enemy, was utterly helpless to avert a catastrophe.

The waggon was finally overturned and the inmates of a dozen hives set at liberty. The waggoner and a lad who was with him luckily escaped without a broken limb, but they were so badly stung about the face and hands that the services of

Dr Saymes had to be obtained, and they are reported to be progressing favourably.

The horse (a valuable animal belonging to Mr Heath) managed to smash the shafts and kick itself free of the waggon; but thousands of bees must have pierced its body – in fact, it was surrounded by a dense cloud of them – and dropped down dead, having been literally stung to death.

The Edinburgh Evening News,
July 30, 1897

'Father Christmas' on Fire

At the Peterborough Infirmary on Thursday Mr A.C. Taylor, the dispenser, was dressed as 'Father Christmas,' with a flowing hirsute appendage of cotton wool, and was distributing the articles from a Christmas tree when the wool beard caught alight enveloping his head in flames. His moustache, eyelashes, and eyebrows were singed off, and his face, ears, and head were badly burnt. It is, however, hoped that his injuries will not be of a permanent character. Fortunately a panic among the inmates was prevented.

The Evening Telegraph and Star, Sheffield,
January 3, 1891

Strange Accident

Seven persons have been dangerously hurt at Glasgow, by an explosion of gunpowder. A deaf and dumb man found a keg in a passage, and took it home; thinking it contained butter. Failing to force it open with a poker, he made the poker red-hot, and proceeded to bore a hole in the keg; the contents were gunpowder. The explosion which followed blew the roof off the house, and every person in the building, except an infant, suffered.

The Carlisle Journal, February 10, 1854

The Tragedy at Sunderland

The appalling catastrophe which occurred at Sunderland on Saturday will send a thrill of horror throughout the kingdom.

Not since the terrible collision on the Thames between the Princess Alice and the Bywell Castle has such an immense loss of life been recorded as the result of a preventable accident; and in the present case the calamity is, if possible, aggravated by the fact that the sufferers are children of tender years, and that their death was one of the most horrible that can be imagined.

No such holocaust of youthful victims has ever been recorded in the annals of our national disasters, and certainly no more heart-rending scenes could be imagined than those which were presented at the Victoria Hall, Sunderland on Saturday evening.

A well-known conjuror, by offering to give his entertainment at a merely nominal charge, had attracted from 1,100 to 1,200 children to the largest hall in the town, to witness an entertainment which has a special attraction to the juvenile mind. Everything passed off well till the close of the entertainment, when the children began to leave the hall.

The little ones, who for the most part were under 12 years of age, were coming trooping down the stairs leading from the gallery in hundreds, little dreaming, we may well suppose, of the awful ending which awaited their afternoon's amusement.

It is stated that a door at the top of the first flight of stairs, through some most unaccountable mismanagement, was only open a space of about 20 inches, so that only one child could pass through at a time.

What followed recalled the terrible catastrophe that occurred at Bell Street Hall on New Year's Day, 1865. The exit becoming blocked, and the youngsters continuing to press from behind, were heaped together in an inextricable mass, piled one upon another in all conceivable forms, and before proper assistance could be obtained nearly 200 had met with a most cruel death. A most sad ending this to what all had expected would prove a pleasant afternoon's enjoyment!

Of course there will be a full inquiry into the cause of this most unfortunate occurrence, and until this has taken place it would not be proper to say who is to blame for the appalling loss of life that has taken place.

The facts, however, so far as they have as yet been ascertained, seem to point to the necessity that still exists for further regulations as to the means of exit from large public halls and places of amusement.

Especially is this the case when the audience consists for the most part or entirely of children. It is hinted, in the reports of the occurrence which have been furnished, that there was not a sufficient number of adults in charge of the multitude of children who were assembled to witness the performance.

This also is a matter that is sure to receive some attention from those who have the care of children committed to them.

The Dundee Courier and Argus, June 19, 1883

✦ FASHION and CLOTHES ✦

~ Preface ~

The day John Hetherington put on his new hat and went for a walk, he caused something of a stir. Children screamed, women fainted, and a boy on an errand was knocked over by the excitable crowd and broke his arm.

The hullaballoo in the centre of London in January 1797 was sparked by nothing more than the sight of Hetherington's silk top hat, 'such a tall and shiny construction on his head that it must have terrified nervous people', said a witness. It was a riotous debut for a design that would become emblematic of sober authority in the century to follow.

After the fops, fribbles and popinjays of earlier eras, fashion in the Victorian age was characteristically muted. Like the straight-laced offspring of hippy parents, the Victorians were rather ashamed of the plunging necklines, elaborate wigs and general stylistic antics of previous, more daring generations.

Modesty became the guiding principle. Modesty and dignity. And if there was room for some gross discomfort too, so much the better. Corsets were worn swoon-inducingly tight. Skirts were the width of a supersized hula-hoop. A lady's daily dress was built up in stages, in the style of a Russian doll.

As for men, they weren't dressed properly until they looked like they had been freshly dipped in a solution of starch. The sole nod to frippery came in facial hair; the unrulier the better, from dundreary whiskers to beards of a length and bushiness to rival a desert-island castaway.

But if the Victorian era was no equal for the punky excess of the eighteenth century, it did at least boast one craze daft enough to match any other conjured up in the entire history of fashion.

It began with an outbreak of rheumatic fever that left the fondly-regarded Princess Alexandra lame. As she was a trend-setter, fashion-conscious women in the capital were soon to be seen affecting a hobble.

They called it the Alexandra Limp, and it spread quickly across the country. 'It is as painful as it is idiotic and ludicrous', wrote an Edinburgh journalist, after spotting three dedicated followers of fashion clump down Princes Street. 'I heard that a fashionable Edinburgh shoemaker, one who carries the royal arms over his shop front, actually made and vended the boots necessary to produce the deformity, and exhibited them in his window, one with a high heel and one without.'

A Word for Crinoline

Some time ago a young lady walking in the country was suddenly attacked by a large and ferocious dog, so that her fate seemed inevitable.

But being amply provided with a crinoline, she soon had recourse to the usual expedient of stooping down, so as to allow the lower portion of her dress to collect around her; and the crinoline, by its enormous stiffness, kept off all the attacks of the animal until assistance arrived.

The Dundee Advertiser,
September 11, 1863

Saved by Her Corset

A tailor shot at Mrs Dove, the wife of his employer, at Faversham, last evening, with a revolver. The bullet struck the region of the heart, but was stopped by the corset steel. The man is in custody.

The Sunderland Daily Echo and Shipping Gazette,
September 25, 1900

Crinoline Accidents

In one case, crinoline has been the means of saving life. At Bristol, the other day, a woman either jumped or fell into the Float at the Stone Bridge, and it was some time before any person came to her assistance. She remained on the surface of the water, however, during that period, by means of her crinoline. She was eventually rescued with grappling irons. Two men who saw her in the water plunged in to save her, but being unable to swim, they narrowly escaped drowning.

We are glad to hear Lady Mildmay is pronounced in a convalescent state, though still, as well as Sir Henry Mildmay, suffering much from the violent kicks of the horse who was frightened by her Ladyship's crinoline, when she went up to the horse-box in the stable. The fearful accident happened at Heckfield Park, Hampshire, the seat of her Ladyship's father, Viscount Elmsley.

Near Carlisle, a party of young people were crowding round beehives, when, in stooping in the vicinity of these, one of the girls' crinolines hooked over the top of the hive, and when the poor girl, ignorant of the fact, walked away, down came the hive, of course.

The whole corps d'armee instantly set upon their unwitting assailant, who, to escape their notice, was obliged to run for it, and eventually to take refuge in a pool of water. She was badly stung.

The Hereford Times, October 5, 1861

The Danger of Jute Chignons

It is reported that a woman died recently in Indianapolis from the effects of the ravages of jute worms, which had entered her scalp from the jute chignon which she had worn for a number of years.

The Dundee Courier and Argus, March 15, 1872

Inkslinging Extraordinary

'Jack the Inkslinger' has been creating an amount of consternation in New York, only second to that of 'Jack the Ripper' in London.

His aim has been to destroy the most beautiful dresses to be seen in the promenades, by throwing violet-coloured ink over them; and so many have been completely destroyed that big rewards have been offered for his capture.

According to the *New York Tribune*, the police believe they have captured him. Their prisoner is John Connors, a tall, lank, beardless Irishman, about 35 years old. He is said to have a roving eye, the expression of which indicates a diseased mind. His wife and four children live in the tenement house No. 443, West Fifty-Second Street. The family came from Ireland.

Connors has been employed every day for some time changing the harness on the car horses, and has finished his work about 10.30pm. On Friday night, Policeman Stafford saw Connors following two women in a suspicious manner at Ninth Avenue and Fifty-Ninth Street. Connors kept close behind them until they turned into a side street. Then he stood for a moment as if uncertain whether to follow them any further or not.

Stafford went up to him and asked him what was the matter. Connors said, 'Nothing.' As he was moving away, Stafford noticed that he put one hand into his coat pocket. The policeman caught the hand and found in it a bottle of violet ink. That was sufficient to cause the arrest of the man.

At the police station more evidence of guilt was found. In one pocket were three bowls of clay pipes. The bowls were stained with violet ink, and one bowl held a small quantity of the fluid. Part of another bowl, which had been broken, was found in one of the prisoner's waistcoat pockets, and two of the pockets were stained with ink on the inside. There was ink on the prisoner's fingers also.

Connors denied that he had thrown ink on women's dresses. He said that he had found his little boy playing with the ink and bowls and had taken them away from him.

His actions led the police to believe that he was partly, at least, insane. His wife and children were questioned and they denied that they had ever seen the ink or the bowls.

Mrs Connors said her husband had been acting strangely and probably was not in his right mind.

The Citizen, Gloucester, July 1, 1890

Actress in Male Attire.
Attempt to Enlist as a Soldier

An extraordinary story was told at the Marlborough Street Police Court, London, today. Harriet Muir, aged 28, described as an actress, staying at Anderton's Hotel, was charged with being in male attire. She appeared in the dock in the clothes in which she was arrested – dark striped trousers, pilot jacket, and wore her hair short.

It appeared that she presented herself yesterday afternoon at St George's Barracks for enlistment as a soldier, and her sex being suspected, she was at once taken before the doctor, and her sex ascertained.

Mr Arthur Newton, for the defence, said the accused ran away about four years ago from her home at Christchurch, New Zealand, where her father was a sheep farmer. She had since maintained herself respectably on the stage, and had been acting at Bristol but finding herself out of employment came up to London last Sunday, and put up at Anderton's Hotel.

She went to London Dock and endeavoured unsuccessfully to obtain a situation as a steward on some vessel going to New Zealand, and then walked to St George's Barracks, and tried to enlist, thinking that in the circumstances that was the best thing she could do.

It was now proposed that her friends in the City should be communicated with and her passage to New Zealand arranged for. She was discharged on this understanding.

The Evening Telegraph and Star, Sheffield, March 6, 1889

Another Woman in Male Attire

A prisoner giving the name of John Bradley was sentenced to fourteen days' imprisonment for vagrancy at Dublin on Saturday. On being directed when in prison to prepare for a bath, the prisoner refused, and when threatened with compulsion the culprit burst into tears, saying she was a woman.

She was subsequently removed to the women's prison. She is a good-looking brunette, aged 24, and says her mother dressed her in boys' clothes from childhood, and when her mother died saw no reason to change her attire.

The North-Eastern Daily Gazette, Middlesbrough, March 18, 1889

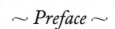

~ *Preface* ~

The story went something like this. Deep in the heart of the woods of Kostroma in Russia, a hunter spied a sudden burst of movement; two monstrous figures moving between the trees.

Returning with back-up, he tracked the beasts to their lair. Like any wild animal, they put up a savage fight when cornered, but the huntsman finally had his prize.

That's how showman P.T. Barnum told the tale, anyway. And whether they believed him or not, the crowds came all the same, eager to see the spectacle Barnum billed as the 'crowning mystery of nature's contradictions', 'the incarnate paradox, for which Science stands confounded and blindly wonders', 'the most prodigious paragon of all prodigies', or, for any-one pushed for time, Jo-Jo, the Dog-Faced Boy.

Jo-Jo was actually Fedor Jeftichew, who had toured the circuses of Europe and Britain with his father a decade before, where they were first advertised as the product of a repulsive liaison between a peasant and a bear, then later as proof of Darwinism, a hiccup in the evolution of mankind.

In truth, Fedor had simply inherited his vodka-swigging dad's chronic condition of hypertrichosis, which obscured their features in great mats of hair.

But truth wasn't really a concern for Barnum, who took Fedor to America in 1884, and worked him … well, like a dog. At the height of his fame he would perform more than twenty shows a day, occasionally growling and barking for the pleasure of the punters.

And there were plenty of them. After the industrial revolution came the recreational one. A series of reforms left people of the late nineteenth century with more time on their hands than the generations before, and more ways to spend it.

Theatres popped up like spring blooms; music halls and working men's clubs too. Parks opened, sports stadiums were built, art galleries and museums flourished and a golden age of literature yielded riches upon riches. But the Victorians were forever drawn to the grotesque, and the fairground mix of hokum, fraud and out-and-out exploitation.

Jo-Jo returned to Britain in 1898 and 1899, as Barnum's vast, eclectic 'Greatest Show on Earth' toured the nation, dropping jaws wherever it went. A piece in the theatrical paper *The Era* in January 1899 ducked out of trying to describe all the acts and settled on listing the 'extraordinary oddities' involved. The moss-haired girl; the lady with a horse's mane; the tattooed people; the human ostrich; the expansionist; the cat orchestra; the Yankee whittler; the Albino dislocationist; Little Peter, the dwarf; the Orissa Twins; the wild men of Borneo; the bearded woman; the card-playing pig; the human pin-cushion; the armless wonder; the legless wonder; the hard-headed wonder; the double wonder; the elastic man; and finally the 'What Is It?'

And What Was It? A bloke from New Jersey, dressed up in a fur suit. 'We've got something for everyone', Barnum used to say. Particularly the gullible.

'The Dog Faced Girl'
How Curiosities are Manufactured

A girl of fourteen, named Watine, who was missing from Roubaix, has been discovered by her parents at the Tourcoing Fair, where she was being exhibited in a booth as a woman with a dog's face.

The showman had cleverly covered the girl's face with gum, to which the hair and ears of a dog were attached. By order of the police, these were washed off, and after the parents had rescued their daughter, the Mayor ordered the booth to be shut up.

The Hampshire Advertiser, Saturday, August 6, 1892

A Chivalrous Cowboy

Austin, Texas, Friday: During a performance given here last night of a sensational border drama, 'Wild Bill,' a cowboy in the audience, carried away by excitement, drew his pistol and fired at the villain in the play. The villain was in the act of abducting the heroine, and the cowboy objected.

Unfortunately, his aim was bad for he missed the villain and shot the heroine through the shoulder. There was considerable excitement in the theatre, and the play was stopped. The young lady is seriously, but not dangerously, wounded.

The Shields Daily Gazette and Shipping Telegraph,
October 9, 1897

Shocking Affair in a Ball Room

A shocking scene occurred at a ball at Thurmaston, near Leicester, on Wednesday night, given by a gentleman of that village to a party of friends.

It seems that the ball had not long begun when the dress of one of the ladies caught fire through being brought into too close contact with the firegrate.

Becoming terrified by her situation she rushed about the room, and ignited the dresses of three other ladies, which, being of such light material, were speedily in a blaze.

Mr Jacques, house-surgeon of the Leicester Infirmary, who happened to be one of the party, aided with others, extinguished the flames as quickly as possible but not before the ladies had been considerably burnt – two of them seriously so. Their injuries were at once attended to, but they are not yet pronounced out of danger.

The scene in the ball-room may be more readily imagined than described. It is hardly necessary to add that the occurrence of such a catastrophe had the effect of bringing the evening's entertainment to an abrupt termination.

The Western Daily Press, Bristol, January 21, 1867

An Extraordinary Occurrence

An extraordinary occurrence took place late on Thursday week on the Great Western Railway.

One of the travellers by the down train, which leaves the Bath station at 20 minutes past ten, was Mr Charles Shaw, who has been performing in the pantomime at the Theatres, Bath and Bristol.

It is believed that he was not tipsy, and it is said that he is a steady, sober man; but he must have been seized with some delirium, for the train had got to within three or four miles of Bristol, when he made a sudden leap through the window of the carriage in which he was riding, and disappeared from his alarmed fellow-passengers.

Of course the train could not be stopped, but upon its arrival at the Bristol station, the officials immediately sent back an engine to ascertain the fate of the man. He was found on the siding, alive, and without having sustained any fracture, but suffering from many contusions and from concussion of his brain. He was at once brought into Bristol and conveyed to the infirmary, where he now lies.

It is a remarkable fact, that in one of the scenes in the pantomime in which he has been playing, the clown, pantaloon, and sprite have to jump through the window of a Great Western Railway train while in motion, and that the scene is then immediately changed to the Bristol Royal Infirmary. It is not improbable that these circumstances might have had some influence on a diseased mind.

The Leeds Intelligencer, February 18, 1854

Lilliputian Exhibition of Tiger Taming

From Paris the other day came a story, half-grotesque and half-revolting, of a cruelly ingenious showman to whom there had occurred the idea of getting up a Lilliputian exhibition of tiger-taming.

He procured four cats, whose bodies he painted orange-tawny, with black stripes, so as to be closely imitative of the hide of *felis tigris*, and then he engaged a little boy, who clad in tights and spangles, was to enact the part of a beast tamer, but who, prior to his appearance in public, was shut up in a cage with the cats and instructed to reduce them to subjection and to teach them a variety of tricks by means of rigorous chastisement.

If, however, the poor little tiger king was provided with a switch, the four Lilliputian tigers had been endowed by nature with a due complement of claws; and they so worried and tore the unfortunate lad that, had he not been able to make his escape from the cage, fatal results might have followed.

He ran shrieking into the street, pursued by his master; but the police interfered, and the Correctional Tribunal may possibly have something very serious to say to the barbarous promoter of Lilliputian tiger-taming exhibitions.

The Illustrated Police News, January 29, 1876

Rival Bands

A serious riot occurred on Sunday in Cork. The disturbance originated in a difference between two bands belonging to the north part of the city. The Blackpool Band accused the Fair Lane Band of receiving money, which they did not divide fairly, and, attacking them, broke their musical instruments.

The members of the latter and their friends took reprisals on Saturday night by attacking the quarter of the rival band and wrecking their houses. On Sunday the riot was resumed with greater vigour. One party gave battle to the other in the street, and for over an hour a fierce conflict raged with stones and other missiles. The whole available police force of the city was summoned to the scene, and the rioters were not dispersed before 11 o'clock. The casualties during the two nights were 40 scalp wounds, including four fractures of the skull. Among the seriously wounded was a policeman named Rooney.

The Western Daily Press, Bristol, May 6, 1879

Pelted with Cabbage.
Scene in a Paris Theatre

An extraordinary scene took place at the Opera Comique, Paris, during the production of M. Saint-Saens' opera 'Phryne.'

The title *role* was given by Mlle. Jeanne Hading, who when she made her appearance on the stage was received with an outburst of hissing and hooting by several persons in the stalls and boxes.

One of these was occupied by a lady, who evidently came provided for the occasion, as she immediately began to throw cabbages, potatoes, and similar missiles at the actress. It is said that Mlle. Hading had captivated the lady's husband, and that, owing to the relations between them, she therefore took this opportunity of revenging herself.

The Midland Daily Telegraph, Coventry, February 24, 1894

Sarah Bernhardt's Leg

Madame Sarah Bernhardt has had a gruesome and startling offer from an American showman. A Paris correspondent says that when she was seriously laid up with a bad leg there was a report that amputation might be found necessary.

This piece of news was promptly cabled to the United States, and the notion at once occurred to a showman to buy, embalm, and exhibit the limb in the event of its being amputated. A large sum was offered, with a share in the profits of the exhibition.

The Citizen, Gloucester, June 16, 1890

A Human Monkey.
Curious Story of a Child's Life

A reporter made enquiries on Tuesday at the offices of the Salvation Army with regard to a report in an American paper, stating that a girl, who was found in a Kentish hop-field dressed in the skin of a monkey, had arrived in New York with a Salvation Army officer.

According to the Salvation Army officers the parents of the child are unknown, but when about two years of age she was stolen by an itinerant minstrel who travelled about all parts of the country. This man, it seems, procured an old skin of a monkey and stuck it on the child, to whom he administered repeated doses of gin, so as to stop her growth. The gin produced this effect, and even now the girl is little bigger than a midget.

In the course of time the skin came to fit the child like a glove. The face and hands only were exposed, and these, never being cleansed, soon became grimy. In this condition it is evident the child remained for over a year before her identity was discovered by Miss Swift, one of the Salvation Army slum officers.

The child was taken by the minstrel all over the country. She was dressed in the usual red coat, and carried a shell, with which she had been taught to beg for alms. She was never washed, and in order that the deception might be maintained her head had been shaved. Her nails grew long, and her hands and feet were so emaciated and dirty that it is marvellous how the discovery of her identity was made at all.

Miss Swift states that in winter the child travelled with a company, made up of men chiefly, who played a sort of pantomime. There were various odd characters in the piece, but the only ones she remembers were the devil and the monkey. The trained monkey was the star performer. She could climb up on a table, going up one of the legs, with as much agility as any real monkey.

The Western Gazette, Yeovil, January 15, 1897

A Perilous Balloon Trip

Three aeronauts, Mlle. Lena Dare, Signor Spelterini, and an assistant, made a perilous ascent from the Clarendonia Grounds, at Leicester, on Saturday evening.

A strong wind prevailed, rocking the balloon very violently. Spelterini and his assistant were in the car, but the lady hung on by her teeth to a trapeze under the car.

The balloon shot away rapidly, swaying the lady most violently backwards and forwards as she was carried rapidly over the town. She, however, stuck to her performance on the trapeze until she disappeared from sight.

The balloon travelled rapidly eastwards, and, owing to the late ascent, darkness was coming on before the aeronauts could descend. An effort was made to alight near Great Dalby, but the grappling-iron failed to hold, and the strong wind carried the balloon bumping along over fields and through hedges for two miles.

To avoid contact with the buildings the balloon had to be lightened to enable it to reascend. At the next descent the grappling-iron held fast, and the party safely alighted. All three were very much shaken and bruised, but otherwise they were uninjured.

The Citizen, Gloucester, September 3, 1888

A 'Strong Man' as a Lodger

On Wednesday in the Westminster County Court, the case of Brackenbury v. Sandow came before Judge Bayley. The plaintiff claimed £4 12s. 6d., for damage done to the ceiling and furniture at 6, Rupert Street, London, by the defendant, known as 'the Strong Man.'

Mr T. Mann, in opening the case, said the defendant (who did not appear) rented some rooms at the plaintiff's house, and after a little time he commenced to practise some feats of strength in the rooms with dumb-bells and heavy weights, with the results that the ceiling of the room below came down.

He stopped practising with the weights, but commenced to use a pistol, with the result that he damaged the wall paper and fired through a picture frame. He also dropped one of the dumb bells on a cabinet, knocking the corner off. Plaintiff gave evidence in support of this statement, and, in answer to his Honour as to what objection he had to dumb-bells, the plaintiff said, 'One of them weighed 320lbs, sir.' His Honour gave judgement for the plaintiff for the amount claimed, with costs.

The Huddersfield Daily Chronicle, November 13, 1890

Uproar in a Paris Theatre

A Paris correspondent telegraphs: A great uproar was caused in the Theatre des Menus Plaisirs on Saturday night. During the performance of what is called a 'revue,' in which the vendors of lying news-sheets were satirised, the audience heartily applauded a scene where a fellow crying out the adventures of a colonel is taken to task by another actor who sings a couplet praising the military.

In the midst of the applause a loud hiss was heard. It proceeded from the front orchestra stalls, where a young man of respectable appearance was seated.

He was remonstrated with by those about him, but, nothing daunted, he continued his hissing, and as the imaginary newsvendor broke away from the grasp of the singer, calling him opprobrious names, the young man stood up and applauded with energy. He was immediately set upon by the persons near him, and was thrashed within an inch of his life.

When rescued by the men of the Guard, his face was covered with blood and bruises, and his clothes were torn to tatters. During the entr'acts, a crowd of the persons attending the theatre tried to get the man out of the police-office. They evidently wanted to kill him for having defended the newsboys in the teeth of the whole house.

The Manchester Evening News,
March 8, 1886

A Singular Incident

A melancholy fracas has occurred at Indianapolis owing to an actor being bitten by a dog.

It seems that there is an actor there of such exquisite proportions that he is known as the Apollo Belvedere. He was walking in the streets the other day and exciting universal admiration by the magnificent proportions of his limbs, when he accidentally stepped on the tail of a terrier dog who happened to come across his path.

The enraged animal immediately turned and bit the actor severely in the calf of the leg. The wounded man, however, stalked on apparently unconscious of the injury he had received until a bystander called his attention to the circumstance.

He immediately stopped, and the utmost sympathy was felt for him and expressed by the spectators until to their amazement and horror they saw flowing from the wound – not a drop of blood – but a thin stream of sawdust.

The incident naturally caused a painful sensation in the city, and was mentioned with kindly regret by one of the local papers. This annoyed the actor excessively, and announcing his intention to chastise the editor he proceeded to the office of that gentleman to carry out his intention; but the muscles of his arms proved as little formidable as the calves of his legs, and after a short and sharp struggle he was ignominiously kicked by the editor out of his room.

Altogether he has sadly fallen in the estimation of the public, and it is understood he contemplates retirement from the stage – at all events for a time.

The Manchester Evening News, June 12, 1873

An Editor Horsewhipped by Chorus Girls

According to a report in the *South Australian Register* there was an exciting scene in a New Zealand newspaper office recently.

It appears that in consequence of strictures on the characters of members of the Gaiety Theatrical Company, published in the *Workman*, of Dunedin, several members of the company went to the office, and, failing to get a satisfactory explanation from the editor, five chorus girls thrashed him and the printers with horsewhips.

The party were ultimately ejected, but they broke the doors and windows, forced their way inside again, and wrecked the premises.

An actor was struck a severe blow on the right eye during the melee in the street. On the following day some members of the company were brought up at the police court, but the charge was withdrawn.

The Edinburgh Evening News, July 11, 1893

The 'Manard Coat' Demonstrations
Shooting Accident at the Canterbury Music Hall

Miss Julie Manard, the wearer of the Manard bullet-proof coat, was struck in the neck by a bullet while being shot at on Saturday evening at the Canterbury Music Hall. She was removed to St Thomas's Hospital, where she is progressing favourably.

In an interview with a press representative the marksman can only attribute the accident to the deflection of the rifle before the bullet cleared the barrel.

It is stated by a news agency that the London County Council is about to take steps for the prevention of the public exhibitions of the bullet-proof coat, on the grounds of the great risk attaching to such exhibitions.

The Pall Mall Gazette, May 28, 1894

Fearful Riot in Leicester.
Coxwell's Balloon Burnt.

On Monday, at the Foresters' Fete, at Leicester, the populace burnt Coxwell's balloon, 'Britannia,' in which the aeronaut had proposed to make an ascent, and they would, in all probability also have killed himself had he not been escorted off the ground by a strong body of police.

It was announced that the balloon ascent would take place at half-past five o'clock, and as the hour approached there was a great rush to see the air-ship, which was then in process of being inflated.

The police were unable to keep back the 'roughs,' and a series of rows was the result, in which serious wounds were inflicted on both sides. One of the policemen, by a blow of a stake on the forehead, knocked down a woman, who lay on the ground bleeding profusely.

This, we trust, accidental outrage, infuriated the mob, who instantly made a most determined attack on the constables.

The scene of riot and confusion was indescribable; and eventually the constabulary were beaten back.

Mr Coxwell was seated in the car of the balloon with thirteen gentlemen, who were desirous to make the ascent along with him. He repeatedly assured the crowd that if they did not desist from violence he would not make the ascent at all. But the mob was too infuriated to listen to any appeals, and Mr Coxwell ultimately pulled the valve rope and allowed all the gas to escape.

The passions of the mob were raised to the highest pitch by this proceeding. They instantly levelled all the barriers, broke into the reserved space, and the cry having been raised to burn the balloon there were plenty of incendiaries to answer to the appeal.

Mr Coxwell was escorted off the ground by a body of police, leaving his balloon a prey to the victorious mob. They gathered rapidly around, cutting the oiled calico, of which the body of the balloon was formed, into shreds; and having taken away as many trophies as they pleased, set fire to the remainder. In the process of cutting up the balloon, several of the rioters sustained severe wounds on the hands and fingers.

After the work of destruction was completed the rioters paraded the town in triumph, and Mr Coxwell, to escape the torrent of popular fury, left Leicester by the first available train.

Several accidents occurred on the London Road, which leads to the Race Course, owing to furious driving; and on the whole, Leicester witnessed a series of riots and disorderly tumult, rarely experienced.

The Nottinghamshire Guardian, July 15, 1864

A Wonderful Parrot

Mrs Mackay, the 'Bonanza Queen,' has, writes a London correspondent, provided during her absence the public of London with a gratuitous entertainment of a most diverting nature.

At her open window in Buckingham Palace Gate is a wonderful green parrot, which attracts hundreds of people every day to hear him talk. The crowd on Sunday was so great that the policeman had to request the people to 'move on.'

'Move on,' echoes the parrot, to the intense delight of the mob. 'Polly, what is o'clock?' asks a man. The parrot, pretending to look at the clock, cries out in answer – 'Half-past five,' and he was right.

I asked him how his mistress was? 'Coming over soon, all right,' replied the marvellous bird. 'How old are you, Polly?' 'Don't know. How old are you?' was the answer, which, of course, provoked great merriment, in which the parrot joined. Asked what day of the week it was, the wretch hopped about screaming 'Sunday; go to prayers. *Ora pro nobis*,' and fell into a paroxysm of laughter which was quite contagious.

The Dundee Courier and Argus, September 20, 1889

Andrian, the Dog-Headed Man, and his Son, Fedor

The likenesses of the two extraordinary creatures on our front page are correct representations of the singular beings now being exhibited nightly at the Metropolitan Music Hall, Edgware Road.

The face of Andrian, the father, is covered with hair, and presents the appearance of one of the lower animals of the creation. He is fifty-five years of age, and has four teeth on the lower jaw and two on the upper – these are the only teeth he ever possessed; he is quiet and unobtrusive in manner, and has been for the greater part of his life a denizen of a Governmental forest, in Russia, called Kostroma.

While in his native wilds he was habited in skins of bears and other animals, and it was with much difficulty that he was prevailed upon to clothe himself in civilised costume.

The hair on his face, forehead, and ears appears in form and structure unlike that which usually grows on human beings.

The boy – his son, Fedor – is four years old; his face is covered with light coloured downy hair, resembling in some respects the soft fleecy wool of a lamb. He has four teeth on the lower jaw, but none on the upper. Fedor is a lively, merry little fellow. Both father and son have been presented at the Russian Court. They have also been exhibited at Paris, where they attracted crowds of curious and wonder-struck people. The dog-headed man and his son are most unquestionably the greatest phenomenon of the age. Whether there are other beings of a similar nature residing in the Russian forest, from whence they come, we are not able to say, but these two are interesting and remarkable in the highest degree.

The Illustrated Police News,
February 7, 1874

ANDRIAN THE DOG FACED MAN AND HIS SON
SINGULAR BEINGS FROM THE KOSTROMA FOREST, RUSSIA

Mock Modesty in Detroit.
Classical Statues to be Draped

It seems from an American cablegram, says a contemporary, that the mock-modesty which led the Americans of some generations ago to breech the legs – or rather limbs – even of their tables and chairs is not yet quite extinct.

Some 'old women' (of both sexes) inhabiting Detroit, supported by all the Presbyterian clergymen in the city, have delivered a solemn protest to the directors of the local art museum to the effect that the nude statues there shown were a corruption and a stumbling block to the youth of the city.

They indignantly demanded that all the statues should be draped, threatening to boycott the institution as a place of immoral resort unless their suggestions were immediately adopted. The directors, before such Horsleian fervour, have given way. They have issued an order that all the nude statuary in their galleries should be dealt with even as the hearts of the petitioners desired. They may as well sell them for tailors' models at once.

The Citizen, Gloucester, July 9, 1890

An Unlucky Musician.
Curious Result of a Fall

A very curious case, says a Paris correspondent, has just been brought before one of the Rouen law courts.

Some time ago a tight-rope dancer was performing at a local music hall when the wire suddenly broke, and she fell from a giddy height right on the unfortunate conductor of the orchestra, who was so overcome by the shock that he fainted, and when he recovered consciousness was found to be both deaf and dumb!

The affair created no little excitement in the Norman town, and a tremendous controversy soon prevailed. The inhabitants, indeed, were divided into two camps – one side inclining to the opinion that the unlucky conductor was only shamming, while the other stoutly and indignantly maintained that there could not be the slightest doubt as to his good faith.

Although nearly two years have elapsed since the accident occurred the unfortunate musician has not uttered a syllable, nor has he shown the most feeble sign that he can hear a word that is addressed to him.

His application for damages, however, has been rejected. In the judgement it is set forth that if he became dumb it was not owing to his 'receiving' the tight-rope dancer on his head, but to the 'saisissement' resulting therefrom, attributable to his excessively nervous temperament.

This judgement is exciting a certain amount of criticism, considerable sympathy being felt in many quarters for the unlucky victim of the music-hall accident.

The Sunderland Daily Echo and Shipping Gazette,
August 1, 1892

The Serious Accident by the Firing of a Cannon Ball

John Holtum, known among the music hall profession as Herr Holtum, was brought up on remand before the Leeds Stipendiary Magistrate, on Tuesday, charged with unlawfully wounding Elijah Fenton, on the 13th inst.

The prisoner is an athlete, and on the evening in question was performing at the Princess Concert Hall, Leeds, his chief feat being that of catching a nine pound cannon ball, fired from a breech-loading cannon.

He challenged any man to perform the same feat, and offered £50 to anyone who could do it. The bills announcing his benefit, which was on the night in question, gave a list of persons who had been wounded in making the attempt in various towns.

Three men came on to the platform to accept the challenge. The first to try to catch the ball was Mr Fenton, but when the cannon was fired it struck him on the head and knocked him down.

He was conveyed to the Infirmary, where it was found that his skull was fractured, and that he had received injuries to his nose. He is still under medical care. The prisoner was committed to the Leeds Borough Sessions, bail being allowed.

The Staffordshire Daily Sentinel, February 25, 1880

Suicide on the Stage

A German actress named Lola Banzolla committed suicide on Sunday before a crowded audience at Cilli in Styria.

She suddenly drew a revolver, and, exclaiming "Tis love which kills me,' shot herself in the breast.

Indescribable emotion mastered the audience at this sensational interruption of the play, and numbers of them sprang on to the stage, from which the mortally wounded actress was shortly afterwards conveyed to a hospital.

The Leeds Times, April 1, 1899

Curious Phenomenon – Shower of Beef

Benicia, California: A shower of meat fell at the barracks in this city at eleven o'clock last Saturday morning.

The sound of the falling bodies resembled hail, and the pieces on examination proved to be *bona fide* beef.

The shower continued two or three minutes, extending over a space 400 yards long, by 100 broad, and the pieces perhaps in amount not less than 100 pounds, varied in magnitude, from the size of a filbert to a hen's egg.

The meat was generally quite fresh, although some pieces were partly dried, as by exposure to the weather, and all had a ragged appearance, as if they had been torn from the bone, and swallowed by birds.

Two opinions exist as to the cause of the phenomenon; one, that a large number of carnivorous birds were above the spot, at such an altitude as to be invisible, and were caused to disgorge by some – perhaps electrical – change in the atmosphere; the other, that the meat had been blown to a great elevation by a whirlwind, whence it descended in the manner described.

The Hertford Mercury and Reformer,
October 4, 1851

The Wild West.
Desperate Fight Between Two Towns.
Making Arsenals of the Churches.

Kansas, Monday: The citizens of Ingalls on Saturday made an attack upon Cimarron town, owing to a dispute as to which place should be the county town.

After a desperate fight the Ingalls men raided the Clerk's office at Cimarron, and carried off the records. Two men were killed outright, and about one hundred wounded. The citizens of Cimarron set out on Sunday to burn the town of Ingalls, but finding the military in possession postponed their revenge.

Both towns are now like two armed camps. Even the women are armed, and the churches have been turned into arsenals. A renewal of the war is expected shortly. Two citizens from the rival towns met on the road yesterday. They promptly fought, one being killed.

The Evening Telegraph and Star, Sheffield,
January 14, 1889

An Incredible Story

The *Indian Daily News* says: Private George Samphier, of the G Company of the 78 Highlanders, saw a poor little girl about five years old drowning in the river Moola at Kirkee, and, jumping in, tried to save her, but the first attempt failed from the way the child clutched him.

The second time she had sunk, and he then dived and brought her to the surface, and managed to get her ashore, when Apothecary Dias recovered her with some difficulty.

Private Samphier helped to keep the people off from crowding the apothecary during the time he was endeavouring to resuscitate the child, and then returned to barracks.

There the officers in command of the detachment, with true British obtuseness, ordered him to be confined to barracks for 14 days for returning late.

The Dundee Courier and Argus,
September 1, 1879

A Strange Journey.
From Vienna to Paris in a Packing Case

Securely packed in a big box, labelled 'This side up,' 'With Care,' 'Fragile,' and other reminders to railway porters, an Austrian tailor named Hermann Zeitung, according to the police report, has come in a train all the way from Vienna to Paris.

The affair seems incredible, but it is none the less an adamantine fact, and yesterday afternoon the daring tailor was sent off from the Eastern Railway Custom House to the Paris Central Police Station.

The following is the true and authentic version of the strange voyage and adventures of Herr Zeitung. He found himself bankrupt in Vienna, but as he was an able cutter, and had invented a new style of lady's riding dress, he thought that by going to Paris he might be able to make capital out of his invention.

He accordingly ordered a large box, lined it well with straw, and got into it supplied with beer, bread, and sausages. A trustworthy friend or assistant, formerly in his employ, wrote the necessary directions on the box, which was then forwarded to the railway station for Paris.

Ingenious Hermann, the tailor, was thus conveyed by the Orient express across Austria, Bavaria, Wurtemberg, and Alsace into France. During nearly 60 hours he suffered purgatorial pains, for he was unable to move, drink or sleep, and could only squeeze a few pieces of bread and meat now and then into his mouth.

Sometimes he felt himself thrown violently on handcarts by porters while being transferred from one carriage to another; at others he was buried beneath a pile of boxes which threatened to crush in his ribs or smash his skull at any moment.

At last, after having undergone a time of indescribable torture, of which probably no one has ever before had experience, Herr Zeitung suddenly found himself longer than usual out of a railway van.

Then he knew that he had arrived at his destination, but the difficulty was now to extricate himself from his narrow wooden prison. He heard voices and people about him at every minute, and consultations were evidently being held over him, or, rather, his box, which was lying by an unusually long time without anybody coming to claim it.

At last he began to sneeze, and heard somebody mutter an exclamation. Then he coughed, and he heard himself tapped overhead.

Suddenly the lid of his case was lifted off, and out he jumped, to the amazement, if not the consternation, of a group of Custom House officials, who uttered a chorus of interjectory exclamations at beholding a veritable 'Jack in the box' in the shape of a stout under-sized man with a brown moustache, and clothes all covered with straw, salute them in a hang-dog manner, and accost them in a language which they did not understand.

The practical *douaniers* soon recovered from their very natural surprise, and taking in the situation they promptly made a prisoner of the sartorial parcel and marched him before their chief officer, who handed Hermann Zeitung over to the police.

At the station the tailor coolly remarked in German that he did not care about the consequences of his actions as he was now in Paris. He also promised the station superintendent to repay him as soon as he could, but all this he will have to settle with the magistrates.

The Nottingham Evening Post, January 18, 1890

A Duel on Bicycles.
Ludicrous Spectacle

A Paris correspondent says a duel on bicycles was fought in the Boulevard Ney late on Saturday night.

A large party of young fellows had been out cycling all day, and were returning home all very hilarious when two of them quarrelled, and decided to settle the dispute by duel with swords on their bicycles.

The two combatants were placed 50 yards apart, and then ordered to charge. They rode at one another at a furious pace, but overshot the mark and failed to meet. Wheeling quickly round they returned to the charge, and this time came together with a terrific shock.

Both were thrown, whilst the seconds who were following behind, also on bicycles, fell in their turn, and were both injured. Neither of the combatants touched the other with his sword, but in falling one ran his weapon into himself and his opponent injured his leg.

The Evening Telegraph and Star, Sheffield, August 17, 1896

An Incredible Story.
A Mad Mayor Bites Several Councillors

A telegram from Paris states: The newspapers on Saturday morning published an extraordinary telegram, which is received with some hesitation, although it gives the name and place.

The story is that, during the sitting of a provincial town council, the Mayor was suddenly seized with hydrophobia, and bit several of the councillors, who are now on their way to M. Pasteur for treatment.

There is, the telegram adds, no means of saving the Mayor's life.

The Huddersfield Daily Chronicle, March 18, 1889

Extraordinary Escape of a Slave

Henry Box Brown, a fugitive slave from Richmond, Virginia, arrived a few days since at Liverpool, by the Constantine packet-ship, from America.

On the 29th of March, 1849, he escaped from bondage in rather a remarkable manner. He was packed in a box three feet long, two and a half feet deep, and two feet wide. Confined in this small space, he was forwarded by railroad and steam-boat from Richmond to Philadelphia, a distance of 350 miles.

The package was directed to one of the leading anti-slavery men in Philadelphia, and was twenty seven hours on the road. The sufferings of the poor fellow may be imagined when it is known that the only accesses for fresh air were through small gimlet holes in the sides of the box; and, although written directions were placed to 'keep this side up,' for more than two hours the box was turned upside down, the runaway slave being for that time with his feet up and his head down.

Brown is a fine intelligent-looking man, about thirty-five years of age. Since his escape from slavery he had earned a subsistence by exhibiting, in the free-states of America, a panorama of some of the appalling scenes resulting from the existence of slavery. He also delivered lectures against slavery, and thus rendered himself very obnoxious to the slaveowners of the States.

Under these circumstances it was not to be wondered that armed with the powers of the Fugitive Slave Bill, an attempt should be made to arrest him. Two such attempts were made, and it was with the greatest difficulty Brown made his escape to this country.

The Nottinghamshire Guardian, November 14, 1850

Yorks v. Westmorland.
Fight on the Border

The Press Association's Kirkby Stephen correspondent reports an extraordinary scene on the Westmorland and Yorkshire border. A large party, representing the Lords of the various manors, met near Sedbergh to ride the boundaries with a county flag. Certain points were in dispute, and the intention of the Westmorland men becoming known, a party of Yorkshiremen proceeded from Sedbergh and disputed their passage. A free fight occurred at Cautley Spout and blood flowed freely, but the Westmorland men ultimately proved victorious and the boundaries were properly asserted.

The Shields Daily Gazette and Shipping Telegraph,
June 25, 1887

Extraordinary Scene at the Aberdeen University

An extraordinary and disgraceful scene was witnessed in Aberdeen, on Wednesday, in connection with the inaugural address of the Lord Rector of the University, Dr Alex. Bain.

The students, who had been refused the use of the Music Hall in consequence of unseemly proceedings on former occasions, pledged themselves to be orderly in their conduct, and thus obtained the use of the building.

They broke their pledge, however, and the meeting was the most riotous that has taken place in Aberdeen for a quarter of a century. The students marched in a body from the university, headed by itinerant musicians, pelting the people in the streets with peas and shoes, and singing ribald songs.

They boarded the tramway cars, pelting the conductors and passengers. On reaching the hall they found the door barricaded, and guarded by a number of stalwart shore porters engaged for the purpose.

After a disgraceful *melee*, the porters were overpowered, the doors were smashed, and the processionists rushed into the hall, causing the greatest alarm among the ladies and gentlemen who had gathered in the galleries.

The scene that ensued was one of the wildest confusion. Everything the rioters could lay their hands upon was thrown about. Peas fell like hail, and squibs were directed at the parties on the platform, several persons being burned with them.

The furniture was broken and thrown about, the noise and disorder became if possible more intense when the Lord Rector appeared, and after one ineffectual attempt to be heard he had to hold the address as read, and retired along with the members of the Senatus and others who accompanied him.

The students then rushed to the various outlets, firing crackers and peas the while, and in the confusion several of the doors were smashed. Some members of the audience sustained slight injuries. After leaving the hall the students reformed in procession, and marched through the streets singing, shouting, and pelting persons with peas and flour. The police did not interfere.

The Manchester Courier and Lancashire General Advertiser,
November 18, 1882

Stop Press

At Maidenhead on Tuesday, the Mayoress of Henley, Mrs Wanker Simmons, was fined 5s and costs for riding a bicycle on the public footpath.

Reynolds's Newspaper, January 19, 1896

Like the claw machine at the fair, newspapers have an unappealing habit of dropping the things they've just picked up. For things, read people.

Many of the men, women and children in these articles slipped straight back into obscurity, casual discards of an industry that hadn't yet got the hang of the art of the follow-up story. But a few reappeared in print, if only because the mechanics of the justice system shoved them back in the public eye.

Susan Cox, whose baby died in her arms as she wandered the streets of London in a fruitless search for her new home (p. 144), was reunited with her husband two days later. He had been in Croydon, searching for work, unaware of the unfolding tragedy. Mrs Cox, an inquest heard, had unwittingly walked past her house several times.

There was a happier ending to the story of Mrs Lewsey and the phantom London hotel (p. 62). She had checked in with her four-year-old son, left him in a room to go shopping, then couldn't find the address again. Nearly a week later, after an appeal in the press, the boy was discovered, being looked after by the owner of the hotel, which was several miles east of the streets she searched. Mrs Lewsey, who had been in ill-health after the death of a child three months earlier, was also robbed while she was staying in London.

The ghastly tale of the Liberals who roasted and ate a dog to celebrate a school board election in West Bromwich (p. 73) turned stomachs across Britain. The original story was broken by the *Birmingham Gazette*. The rival *Daily Post* sent a reporter to the pub where the election feast had been staged, and heard a markedly different account. Three men had arrived at the inn with a dog, claimed the landlord. First they tried to sell it, but killed it when there were no takers. Before they buried the body, a man cut off one of the legs, the landlord said, and there was some 'very disgusting larking with the limb' before it was chucked into the fire. One of the three men was a Tory, said the *Post*, a paper edited by one of the founders of the National Liberal Foundation. The *Gazette* was staunchly Tory. Make of all that what you will.

With mouths agape in Shropshire in November 1883 at the supernatural antics of servant girl Emma Davies (p. 187), the *Daily News* sent a reporter along to investigate. The teenager soon confessed it was all a trick, saying the other servants had put her up to it. 'The little girl was hysterical at first but by-and-by she showed us how she made a bucket jump and a chair retreat at the double', said the paper. 'It was all effected by a slight jerk of the hand, and when once we knew there was nothing supernatural to be expected, it seemed very commonplace. The most remarkable part of this so-called mystery is the successful hoodwinking of the local public, and the more than nine days wonder which has been caused.'

Thirteen years on from the Regent's Park ice disaster of 1867 (p. 235), when 40 people drowned in water up to 12 feet deep, the calamity claimed one more victim. The father of a girl who had died took his own life after being 'low-spirited for years'.

In 1886, the ice broke again, with 100 skaters plunged suddenly into the water. But after the first tragedy, the depth of the lake had been reduced to around four feet. All that was lost this time round was a number of hats.

The startling Dr William Price (p. 176), the druid arrested on a Welsh hilltop as he tried to burn the body of a dead baby, was a true eccentric: a champagne-quaffing, anti-smoking vegetarian with an inclination for nude picnics, who once fled the country dressed as a woman after instigating a Chartist revolt. It was his own son's body he tried to burn that day in 1884: little Iesu Grist (Jesus Christ, in Welsh), fathered by Price at the age of 83 with his twentysomething housekeeper. He successfully defended himself at Glamorganshire Assizes in Cardiff, dressed in a white robe with a fox head-dress, and was discharged. The case paved the way for the act that legalised cremation in Britain.

The tragedy at Sunderland's Victoria Hall, which claimed the lives of 183 children, forced a change in the law that required all emergency exits to open outwards. Two inquiries were held, but no one was held responsible for bolting the door shut. The memorial to the victims in Mowbray Park was vandalised in 2009.

The crushing truth about Wanker Simmons, alas, is that she never existed; it was nothing more than a newspaper cock-up. The Mayoress of Henley was actually Mrs W. Anker Simmons.

INDEX

Also available:

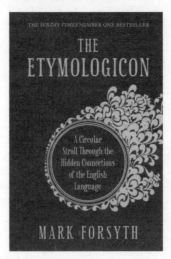

The Etymologicon

A Circular Stroll Through the Hidden Connections
of the English Language

The *Sunday Times* Number One Bestseller

'I'm hooked on Forsyth's book … Crikey, but this is addictive'
—Matthew Parris, *The Times*

What is the actual connection between *disgruntled* and *gruntled*?
What links church organs to organised crime, California to the
Caliphate, or brackets to codpieces?

As heard on BBC Radio 4, *The Etymologicon* – which springs
from Mark Forsyth's Inky Fool blog – is an occasionally ribald,
frequently witty and unerringly erudite guided tour of the
secret labyrinth that lurks beneath the English language. It takes
in monks and monkeys, film buffs and buffaloes, and explains
precisely what the Rolling Stones have to do with gardening.

ISBN 978-184831-453-5

£8.99

The Horologicon
A Day's Jaunt Through the Lost Words of the English Language

'A magical new book … Forsyth unveils a selection of obsolete, but oh-so-wonderful words'—*Daily Mail*

'*The Horologicon* lists many of the fabulous, obsolete gems of our language'—Carol Midgley, *The Times*

As heard on BBC Radio 4, *The Horologicon* (or book of hours) gives you the most extraordinary words in the English language, arranged according to the hour of the day when you really need them.

From Mark Forsyth, author of the bestselling *The Etymologicon*, this is a book of weird words for familiar situations. From *ante-jentacular* to *snudge* by way of *quafftide* and *wamblecropt*, at last you can say, with utter accuracy, exactly what you mean.

ISBN 978-184831-598-3

£8.99